BEFORE THE THUNDER SOUNDS

"Poems to Empower the Soul"

VOLUME 1

RANDY CONWAY

PERCUSSION

Randy Conway Poems
Published by
Percussion Films, llc
Copyright © Randy Conway, 2017

ISBN-13:
978-0692930144 (Before The Thunder Sounds)

ISBN-10:
0692930140

Cover design by
Jeffrey Mardis
Adelie Cox

Printed in the United States of America

PUBLISHER'S NOTE:
While the author has made every effort to provide accurate telephone numbers, Internet addresses and other contact information at the time of publication, neither the publisher nor the author assumes any responsibility for errors, or for changes that occur after publication. Further, publisher does not have any control over and does not assume any responsibility for author or third-party Web sites or their content.

Randy Conway Poems
P.O. Box 157
Halltown, MO 65664
Randyconwaypoems.com
Email: Randyconwaypoems@gmail.com

Published by
Percussion Films, LLC
P.O. Box 282
Mount Vernon, Mo 65712

TABLE OF CONTENTS

Dedication

Acknowledgement

Introduction

CHAPTER 1

CHAPTER 2

DEDICATION

To my biggest fan ever; my mother.
You would be bustin' at the seams.

Charlotte Naomi Conway

September 6, 1933 – June 9, 2017

ACKNOWLEDGEMENTS

Reading the introduction and acknowledgments is a task I usually leave for last. My wife Robin, on the other hand, reads a book from the front cover to the back cover in that order. After taking on this project I will probably change my reading habits. This is my very first attempt at putting together a book of my poetry and I had no idea what an undertaking it can be and how many people become intricate and important parts of making it all come together. Most Christian books appropriately give thanks first to our Savior, Jesus Christ. I will do so also and for so many reasons. First, because He saved me; secondly, because of His great patience and willingness to wait for me to realize that I needed Him; and lastly because of the absolutely miraculous and amazing way God just kept bringing the right people at the right time into my life in order to get me to this place.

I could write an entire book on the influence Steve Quayle has been on my life and my poetry. Thanks for being the first person that I wasn't married to or related to that saw something of worth in my poems and for posting them on your website, stevequayle.com. Thanks for all the advice along the way. Many times while you were on the Hagmann and Hagmann Report, the Holy Spirit inspired a poem through your words. I immediately commenced writing and you shared it live on the air. Wow, what a multi-tasker! Especially, I thank you for the confirmation you shared to get things going. I haven't moved as fast as you — few writers do! My gratitude to you for everything you've done to get me to this point. Your straightforward candor and honesty is a rare find today.

Thanks, Steve, for showing others the value you saw in my work! And, I'm still amazed by our providential meeting in a random restaurant.

I'd also like to thank Joe Ardis Horn who extended such a gracious hand of friendship and gave an entire day of his time to help me move forward. Thanks for the realization that, "I am not that guy." There is no way to express how much of an impact that Joe and Tom Horn, their family and the Skywatch TV family have had on me. Thanks again, Joe!

Thanks also to Michael and Meranda Snyder who also saw value in the content of my poetry; Meranda then shared it on her website, www.whygodreallyexists.com. Thanks for the tips, advice and emails, Meranda.

Thanks to author, film maker and screenwriter, Darrel Campbell. For someone who has 50 projects going on all at once, you still took the time to take on another one. Saying "thanks" doesn't seem quite enough. God gave me the poetry and I had the desire to share it as best I could, thanks to those already mentioned in this forward. But, I didn't have the ability to start a book because I didn't know where the starting point was. Thanks for bringing your know how and your entire Percussion Publishing team into a very niche ministry to help us get here. Thanks Pam, Adelie Cox, the Campbell brothers, Casey, Brock, Brett as well as Steve Snyder, Janie Doss, Erin Turner, Jeffrey Mardis — and I don't even know who all else you've had involved — but we now have a Website, YouTube Channel, Facebook page and this book, quick, fast and in a hurry. Thanks for helping an old friend. We've come a long way from "You're a Good Man Charlie Brown."

It is amazing how many people have played small and large parts with friendship, hands-on help, support and confidence in my writing. Bill and Regina Cameron deserve my thanks for their support, friendship and keeping watch over our business so I could devote more time for this work.

I must extend a special thanks to my dad, Reverend Hubert Conway, my brother, Rick, and my sisters, Cheryl, Marty and Teresa and their families. I would name all of my extended family but I would kill another tree using so much paper. Suffice it to say that the prolific Conway family is a constant support of this dream. Thank you from the bottom of my heart.

Thank you to the readers and listeners of the poems. Your comments, emails and posts keep me enthused about the creative blessings He is giving me. I am blessed by Him and by you.

Finally, I save the best for last. My wife, Robin, is my biggest supporter and sees things in my work that I don't see. Thanks for always reading another poem! Your watchful eye makes me look smarter than I am. I find that out when I'm too impatient and I send poems without your proofreading them! Your faith has strengthened my faith, your confidence in me has given me confidence when I didn't have any, and your wisdom is my blessing. Thanks for sharing your life with me and for sharing my excitement for this book and the ones to follow. I did the easy part; I just wrote down what God was inspiring inside of me. You have done the hard part; spending hours checking my work before it went to Darrel. We could not be more opposite or better suited for each other.

INTRODUCTION

BEFORE THE THUNDER SOUNDS. Have you ever seen a lightning flash and then started counting … "one-thousand-one, one-thousand-two, one-thousand-three" and so on until you hear the thunder clap or roll across the sky? I was always told that the number of seconds between the lightning flash and the thunder sound is how many miles away the lightning strike is. I don't think that is true, but I still find myself counting occasionally. Sometimes, when you see the lightning, you can hardly count a second before you hear a loud clap of thunder. Other times, you may see the lightning and then count several seconds before you hear the deep rumble in the distance. Whatever the case may be, there is an interval between seeing the lightning and hearing the thunder. After seeing the lightning, you are in a state of expectation as you wait for the thunder because you KNOW it is coming. That's where we are today in the prophetic time clock. The lightning (the signs foretold in the Scripture) has struck and now we're counting the seconds before the thunder (The Day of The Lord) sounds. With expectation we are living in that very short interval.

The words of prophecy from Scripture can be confusing and frightening. Many who teach or preach on the "end times" are accused of fear mongering in order to sell prepper supplies. For the most part, that is like calling a proven or factual event a "conspiracy theory" because people then automatically ignore the event. Not all people sharing the unfolding of prophecy are selling anything, rather they are sharing the free gift of God which Satan will quickly call fear mongering in order to deafen the ears of those being warned. I do not want to be guilty of spreading doom and gloom, but I will not fail to warn for fear of what others think about me. I also do not want to be guilty of not telling you that God sent His Son so that you may have eternal life to come and that you may have life in abundance now. This volume of poems deals with the "end times" but not by way of opinion or speculation, but by adherence to what the Bible itself tells us will happen in the last days. What to look for, what events will take place, what the warning signs are and how to escape the coming judgments. What it does not tell us is when the "Day of the Lord" will be. In fact, it tells us no man knows the day or the hour when Christ will return.

These messages in poetry, though sometimes intense, always share the truth that God is our shield and our shelter. The Good News is in the prophecies as well as the warnings. If you live in fear of the warnings, then perhaps a soul check is in order; according to the apostle Paul speaking to Timothy, "We have not been given a spirit of fear but a sound mind." A sound mind wants to know what the warnings are and what the escape route is. The escape route is Jesus. I pray the poems within this book will cause lost men to consider what is coming and seek the salvation offered in the person of Jesus Christ. As you read, you will soon see that you will not survive those things the Bible warns of without a Savior. To the believer, I pray that these verses awaken your soul to the importance of telling others that Jesus is standing at the door waiting to come in. If you don't let Him in, what is coming will break down the door.

"One-thousand-one, one-thousand-two, one-thousand-three…"

BEFORE THE THUNDER SOUNDS

CHAPTER 1

A CALL TO ARMS, A CALL TO ARMS

This poem is birthed from the results of the 2016 Presidential Election and the following biblical references: "Blow the ram's horn in Zion, sound the alarm on My holy mountain..." (Joel 2:1a) See also Jeremiah 4, Ephesians 6: 10-19 and Deuteronomy 30:19.

A CALL TO ARMS, A CALL TO ARMS
by Randy Conway
Copyright © 2017

Sound the Alarm, Yes, Sound the Alarm!

A Call to Arms, Yes, a Call to Arms.

For years the Watchmen have warned of things yet far away,

Now the alarm is sounding for that which is upon us today.

Destruction upon destruction for the whole land is spoiled;

The people have become foolish and in evil are embroiled.

O my soul the sound of trumpet, the alarm of war.

What vials have been opened; what from them will be poured?

Blow the trumpet in Zion and sound an alarm in My Holy Mountain;

The works of the nations have been seen and the sins of the people counted.

Let the priests and the ministers of the Lord now weep.

We did not keep His statutes and now the tares are more than the wheat.

Many believe we have now won a great battle and have folded their hands to sleep,

But we have not as yet even entered into battle, so beware the war upon us creeps.

America has but chosen a man for office and how he leads we are yet to see,

And too many deluded by their bondage believe their chains make them free.

America has awakened briefly before, only to hit the snooze and return to our sleep,

Thinking there is peace and safety when there is no safety and there is no peace.

We have ignored the promise of blessing and curse for those that divide God's land,

And are there not 70 nations desiring to implement their coveted two state-plan?

Now is the time to put on the raiment proper for the conflict.
Time to put on the whole armor that Yahuah provided us with,
Knowing the weapons of our warfare are NOT carnal or
hidden in the shadows,
But mighty through God to the pulling down of strongholds.

Strongholds that have been built for centuries;
Ruled and protected by powers and principalities
Possessing many different modalities using multiple
personalities,
Commonalities, nationalities and political formalities to insure
their finality.

That finality being known by many different names,
But ignored by many, and those who expose it are shamed.
Called conspiracy theorist if you expose the New World Order
And while we sleep the enemy marches ever forward.

Some say we have received a reprieve at this moment.
I say we have an opportunity and if we squander it we will
lament.
For too long we have been found wanting when in the balance
we were weighed.
It is time to fold our hands, not to sleep but to fervently pray.

Many terrible things are ready to be released upon mankind;

How you fair will depend upon with whom you are aligned.

In the midst of the darkness will burn Revival's Fire;

To seek a Great Awakening is that to which we must aspire.

The Fire will light the way for those who have called upon the Living God for sight.

It will be a Refiner's Fire, but those unprepared and unrepentant will face an awful plight.

Those things the Watchmen warned about haven't gone away;

That is why the bells are ringing and the alarm goes out today.

This is a Call to those who claim His Name for revival, for repentance and to pray.

The enemy hasn't given up rather they are gearing up to escalate the fray.

Sound the Alarm, Yes, Sound the Alarm.

This is a Call to Arms, a Call to Arms.

The land before us has been like Eden the beautiful garden,

But behind us it will be desolate if our hearts remain hardened.

We cannot claim that our hearts are not granite and hard as stone,

When the unborn babes cry out from where their discarded bodies are thrown.

We cannot claim we are not stiff-necked when Truth is
trampled in our streets.
We cannot claim our consciences are not seared when artists
and leaders hold spirit feasts.
Destruction upon destruction is cried, for spoiled is the whole
land;
It is time for tearing down, for building up and upon our knees
to take our stand.

What blessings or what curses lie before the people today?
Has not life or death been set before us as the Scriptures say?
Choose life that both thou and thy seed may live;
No greater warning, or opportunity, could Yahuah give.

Let him who has an ear to hear answer the Spirit's call.
The Principalities and Powers are inciting a terrible squall.
It is time to Sound the Alarm, Yes, Sound the Alarm.
Do you hear the Call to Arms, the Call to Arms?

A DAY OF BLESSING AND CURSING

This poem comes from the many references to the "Day of the Lord." "The sun will be turned to darkness, and the moon to blood, before the great and awe-inspiring day of the Lord comes. And it will be that everyone who calls on the name of the Lord will be saved..." (Joel 2:31-32a) See the book of Joel, Isaiah 13, 14 & 30, Ezekiel 3:16-19 and Revelation.

A DAY OF BLESSING AND CURSING
by Randy Conway
Copyright © 2017

Woe, woe, woe to those upon the earth; all who dwell upon the land;

Those who belong to the Most High God should seek shelter under His Hand.

The covering of Heaven is being swept away and it will be Satan's time;

Even some of those protected will be taken and there will be no more warning signs.

God's love will never waiver, His love will never cease.

Hear the Word of the Lord your God as to His servants He does speak.

There is no escaping judgment for it comes from God Most High.

For those lost in lust, in ignorance and confusion, bow your heads and cry.

The time for hearing is now upon all men.

The time of judgment is very close at hand.

The time for men to see has in fullness now arrived.

The "hearing" and the "seeing" will be among those who survive.

The Watchmen who speak not the Truth will be guilty of man's blood.

The Watchmen who have warned in Truth will be found guiltless, judged in love.

There is a call to those who fear the Lord; how can men hear unless the Word is preached?

The work of the Kingdom is made clear and the Word must be spoken until all are reached.

Blessed is the man who is covered by the shed Blood of the Lamb.

Blessed is the man whose name is printed upon God's Hand.

Blessed is the man whose name remains in the eternal Book of Life,

But woe to the man who rejects the Blood; his destiny will be strife.

Woe upon Woe upon Woe is coming upon the earth.

Fear not, this Woe is the call to those who have received the second birth.

Rather fear the Lord your God for He is mighty beyond a man's imagination.

Alas, the fear of the Lord is gone for the people revel in degradation.

The seals will be broken and the scrolls will be opened,

The trumpets will surely sound; the Word of God has spoken.

Attacks and terror will be unleashed and the people will not escape;

Riots and war will be uncontrolled, the children will die and the women raped.

Money will be a memory of days that were in the past

And the earth will shake to its very core; how many men will last?

Last through the storms that will prevail as the world is in travail;

It will be raining fire and hail and now too late men pray to no avail.

Sickness will overcome untold numbers of mankind.

Darkness will envelope us and the light we will not find.

Take heart believer for God has not forgotten and His promises
are true;
His Light will be among the remnant and every morning His
mercies come brand new.

He will provide a refuge; for the faithful there is hope.
The unbeliever will be lost and in darkness he will grope.
Reaching for a hand to rescue him, but it cannot be found;
The time for rescue is before the storm not after the thunder
sounds.

God will judge the deeds of men and He will judge the
churches too.
The line in the sand is drawn and it runs between the pews.
A sword will pierce a mother's heart breaking it in two,
And tears will run like rivers before the Day of the Lord is
through.

We are not to be afraid for He is the First and the Last and He
is the Living One.
Though He once was dead, He is alive forevermore and in Him
all victory is won.
He is the Alpha and the Omega, He is the Beginning and the
End.

He is coming soon with rewards and judgments according to our sin.

For the reborn men all sins are gone; Calvary washed them all way.
Their robes are white giving them right to enter through the narrow
way.
But all will still be judged and rewarded according to what each man
held or what he forsook.
Blessed is he who reads and keeps the words of prophecy found in
God's Holy Book.

The minds of men are given over to their own confusion;
The masses living now under a strong delusion.
Cry out for the innocent, weep for them for there will be no shelter;
The scoffers are lost in a world of perplexity and helter-skelter.

The time for preparation is nearly past;
It is time to pray, it is time to fast.
The covering of Almighty God has now been lifted;
It is a time like no other when men will be sifted.

Be alert for the Day of the Lord is near;
Be prepared for that Day will be severe.
Behold for the hour is now upon you, not someday soon;
Trust, Hope, Watch, Repent for He is coming soon.

A MAN AMONG THE MYRTLE TREES

This poem is taken directly from the biblical account in Zechariah 1:7-17. "I saw during the night a man riding a red horse. But he was standing among the myrtle trees that were in the ravine, and behind him were red, sorrel, and white horses." (Zechariah 1:8) Also see Zephaniah 3, Habakkuk 1 and Revelation 6 & 8.

A MAN AMONG THE MYRTLE TREES
by Randy Conway
Copyright © 2017

There was a time when a man riding a Red horse stopped and

stood among the Myrtle trees.

Behind him came more Riders on a Red horse, a Brown, and a

White horse, there were three.

The Riders were sent with a specific plan

To ride through the earth observing man.

They reported to the Angel of the Lord their observations

Of the condition of the world and the enemies infiltrations.

What if the Riders were once again to mount their steeds

To ride the earth and again report to heaven what they see?

They would see Molech rising up and calling out for blood

And man has provided through abortion a sacrificial flood.
They will see leaders and governments rise with evil enticements
And men worship them as idols and become their idol's sacrifices.

They will see that which is unbearable to see
As man has hastened into perversion and extreme debauchery.
Flesh has become a commodity, a thing to be bought and sold;
Minds of men are now deluded while the church is growing cold.

The Riders are forced to look as Truth is traded for perverse lies
And those who cling to Truth are ridiculed, harassed and even die.
Selfishness reigns in hearts of men seeking to satisfy their greed;
Filling their own pockets while pretending to meet the children's needs.

Now if these Riders returned to the Lord to report all that they had found,

The result would be throughout heaven the echo of trumpet
sound.

Then, four bound angels will be released who have waited for
this very hour.

That hour is upon us and we soon will know God's wrath and
see these angels' power.

The nations will rise together in an arrogant and futile attempt
at war,

But God will cut off the nations and their strongholds and
cities will be no more.

Look at the nations, watch the armies and then be utterly
amazed,

For God will do something beyond belief and we are living in
that day.

We cannot see in the dimensions of the spirit all the horsemen
that ride the skies;

The Riders of the Apocalypse are riding now descending from
on high.

The call is clear, the time is near and repentance should be our
cry.

Great promises await the people of God but first we will be
tried.

The Church must now prepare and spotless She must become,

For heaven's final Rider is ready and quickly He will come.

Even now He sits upon His steed sharpening His Sword.

Soon He will come to claim His Bride, the Almighty Lord of Lords.

COMING BACK

This poem references the many strange descriptions of creatures, beasts and the four horsemen of the Apocalypse as detailed by John the Revelator in the book of Revelation. "He who testifies to these things says, 'Surely, I am coming soon.' Amen. Even so, come Lord Jesus!" (Revelation 22:20)

COMING BACK
by Randy Conway
Copyright © 2017

Seven heads, feathers, fur and wings

A beast with horns and unseen things.

Horses and riders in the sky

A man who's killed but doesn't die.

Vials and lamps upon their stands

Seals and scrolls, I don't understand.

Days of weeks and weeks of years

The unknown words can cause us fear.

But I don't fear the coming Day

I lift my hands and voice in praise,

For long ago in Bethlehem

Fear was banished with good will to men.

These things were written so that we would learn

That the King of Kings will soon return.

This writing of Apocrypha is used to state the fact

That Jesus Christ is Lord of all and He is coming back!

DARKNESS FALLS ACROSS THE LAND

*This poem was birthed from a line that came to my dear friend,
Steve Quayle. He requested that I complete the poem from the
word he received, which was, "Darkness falls across the land
as the Devil himself plays his final hand." Steve then posted
the finished result on his website: www.stevequayle.com. "Woe
to those who call evil good, and good evil; who exchange
darkness for light, and light for darkness; who exchange bitter
for sweet, and sweet for bitter!" (Isaiah 5:20)*

DARKNESS FALLS ACROSS THE LAND
by Randy Conway
Copyright © 2017

Darkness falls across the land

As the Devil himself plays his final hand.

He is ready to implement his ultimate plan

To establish his own kingdom and rule supremely over man.

The darkness is coming and it truly will fall,

In black viscid streams slowly it will crawl.

Crawling across the sky and across the earth

An exploding darkness as it touches the earth.

The darkness will become a treacherous tempestuous storm

Engulfing everything in its path; a black and swirling swarm.

In the hands of the Devil are the cards that he will play;

Those embracing the darkness by the Dark Prince are swayed.

The ignorant don't realize there is power in the darkness.

It will overcome them with a merciless, ravenous starkness.

The kingdom of the Beast as told by John the Revelator

Is a kingdom of darkness ruled by the Great Abominator.

A Black Awakening will be birthed in this dark affliction,

Revealing the men who love the dark; it is their maleficent addiction.

The words of Solomon say darkness is eaten by the fool;

Men will know not upon which they stumble when the darkness rules.

Woe to the men who call good evil and evil good;

They will wish to recant if only they could.

But once the darkness has fallen their chances are few,

For a great delusion will hide their minds from what is true.

Woe to the man who calls the light darkness and the darkness light;

For the Accuser of man is there to intensify man's plight.

The days of darkness are not far away;

The Devil is ready for his final play.

We were warned we would battle the rulers of the darkness of this world.

Powers and spiritual wickedness; in the darkness their presence is unfurled.

The dangers of the darkness are frightening, mysterious and unnamed;

It is in blackest darkness that the Fallen Ones have long been chained.

How have we come to this place where men are lovers of the dark?

Is it not as the days when Noah toiled building the great ark?

The darkness will consume all that it touches

And men will be tormented by its evil clutches.

But I know One of whom the darkness is under His feet;

By His power all the stones of darkness He alone can keep.

And though the darkness is thick and is infested with gloom

And is the wandering place of the Serpent, whose head is plumed,

This One I know can change the impenetrable darkness into Light.

He will overcome the darkness by the Power of His Might.

"As bright as the sun," the Revelator says in describing His Face.

He Himself is Light, and darkness and light cannot occupy the same space.

To play his final hand the Devil will be allowed
And Judgment will come with the dark and swirling clouds.
Know this, people of God, that in Judgment God is highly exalted
And not by our might or power, but by His Spirit will the darkness be assaulted.

And suddenly we realize this darkness is the "Day of the Lord;"
It is the judgment of God and His swift and terrible sword.
Darkness should not be in the walk of the follower of Christ,
For we have been called out of darkness into His Glorious Light.

What will the result of these Days of Judgment be?
Will you be cast into outer darkness for all eternity?
We will overcome the darkness by our Testimony and the Blood of the Lamb,

While the world is made a prisoner of the darkness that descends upon the land.

Yes darkness falls across the land
And the Devil will play his final hand.
Are you prepared for the events that lie beyond our sight?
Can you face the darkness because you are a bearer of the Light?

Men will either overcome the darkness because they have repented,
Or by darkness be overcome because to darkness they have relented.
For a season darkness will have its way
And Satan is ready his final hand to play.

DARKNESS GROWS

Carroll Quigley, in his work, "The Anglo-American Establishment," refers to an invisible secret society that is committed to Arcanum, which is defined as a secret or a mystery. This is a reference to the "Deep State" or "Shadow Government." "The fourth angel sounded, and a third of the sun was struck, and a third of the moon, and a third of the stars, so that a third of them was darkened. A third of the day had no light, and likewise a third of the night." (Revelation 8:12)

DARKNESS GROWS
by Randy Conway
Copyright © 2017

Light is slipping away and darkness is steadily growing;

Faith is slipping away while evil seeds we're sowing.

Men now acclimated to and embrace the growing darkness;

Delusions seize their minds and their hearts are gripped by hardness.

Soon the light will be no more and in the darkness dangers loom;

With drawn curtains to be unseen men gather in a darkened room.

The sun will not light the way and our pathway will be dark;

Evil plans are drafted and on the final journey we have embarked.

Within the darkness fear is nurtured and an impending terror's grown;
Within the darkness a pandemic grows unlike any man has known.
Within the darkness the tempest of nature has begun to churn.
Within the darkness intercessors are at work, praying men will learn;

Praying the evil plans of evil men will not prevail;
The wretched pedophilic plans for evil that Satan birthed in hell.
Now from the darkness grows a famine, can you hear the hungry cry?
And God says, "You have not returned to me," and He questions why.

From the darkness comes a mighty wind blowing across the land,
Destroying all that is in its path; devastation on every hand.
And God says to the man, "You have not returned to me."
From the darkness He has called to us while we refuse to hear or see.

Out of the darkness the water rises and there comes a massive flood.

Men seem hungry now for human flesh with a lust for spilling blood.

God cries out again to man, "You have not returned to Me,"

While rulers sit in darkened rooms, nations planning in futility.

With intensity a fire burns inside the darkness, the flame it yields no light;

And God says, "You have not returned to Me and yet I offer sight."

Inspired by darkness the plans of men become the plans of war,

But when the war is realized their planning will be no more.

The labor pains are growing closer, the Bible predicts our destiny

The cry of Heaven now sent to Earth, "The time is now! Return to me."

The darkness will be dispelled by an everlasting Light;

There will be no need of the sun by day nor the moon at night.

The Light of the World has conquered darkness and the plans of Satan's hordes;

With bowing knees all tongues confess that Light is the Lord
of Lords.
Those who answered the call as God cried out, "Return to
Me,"
Will escape eternal darkness, living with the Light for all
eternity.

Sadly many believe they will never see the darkness because
they will be snatched away,
And while it's true that Yeshua is returning, who can know the
hour and who can know the day?
Our eternity can be certain; the end has been prophesied and
will not be swayed,
But the darkness must come first; now is the time that people
must humble themselves and pray.

DENIAL

I received an email from Steve Quayle asking me to pray about writing something regarding those who remain in denial. Steve is often an inspiration when I read or listen to him, but his prompting is indeed something very special to me. In Proverbs 22:3, we're told that a prudent man foresees evil and hides himself, but the simple continue on and suffer the consequences.

"Then they will call on me, but I will not answer; they will seek me early, but they will not find me. Because they hated knowledge and did not choose the fear of the Lord, they would have none of my counsel and despised all my reproof. Therefore they will eat the fruit of their own way, and be filled with their own devices." (Proverbs 1:28-31) "But whoever listens to me will dwell safely, and will be secure from fear of evil." (Proverbs 1:33)

DENIAL
by Randy Conway
Copyright © 2017

Those who walk in the company of Denial

Will fall in the face of the coming trials.

Those who abide in the Truth will stand

Unmoved by the enemies' evil plans.

A proverb states that the wise man sees trouble from afar;

While the wise are seeking refuge, the fools just wish upon a star.

The wise receive a warning and by lies are not beguiled,

While fools will scoff the warning holding on to their Denial.

Scoffers have always rejected the warnings of the Lord;

Mockers killed the prophets and crucified the Living Word.

Today, they mock the Watchmen who warn of our downward spiral,

Bringing judgment on themselves; it's the fruit of their Denial.

To deny the Truth is the forfeiting of your life.

Because Jesus is the Truth, you are denying Jesus Christ.

The fool believes that Truth is bent to suit his style;

But a day of judgment is upon us when the fool regrets Denial.

The fool hath said in his heart, "There is no God,"

So when the Watchman warns we shouldn't think it odd

That the foolish call the Watchman's words "doom porn" or "maniacal,"

But their unfounded claims will by Truth be shamed along with their Denial.

Awakening to the hour in which we live we must seek His face,

Crying for forgiveness and praying for His grace.

We must continue in our warnings even when reviled,

Praying all will trust in Christ and abandon their Denial.

Those who abide in Truth, with Jesus they will stand,
Prepared for battle in the armor of God against Satan's evil
plans.
For those who march against the Truth in the company of
Denial,
There will be no Rock on which to stand and they will fall in
the face of trial.

These words are not written to wound or condemn,
They are but a warning before opportunity ends.
For even the elect may be deceived by listening to Belial
And the result of great delusion is to cling unto Denial.

DISASTERS AND DIVERSIONS

This poem came to my mind during the 2012 World Series and also while watching the daily news. As far as I can tell nothing much has changed in four or five years except the debt is greater, the protests are louder, the riots and unrest more frequent, the weather more unpredictable, persecution of Christians more prolific and the return of our Savior seems closer than ever before.

DISASTERS AND DIVERSIONS
by Randy Conway
Copyright © 2017

Governments are in constant turmoil and another dictator dies,

The sound of truth is sadly drowned by the mobs loud cries.

Unrest abounds around the world, who will be the next to fall,

While all America idly waits to hear the umpire say, "Play Ball."

Brave soldiers lying wounded, their blood shed on foreign soil;

Before the end of current conflicts, in new wars we are embroiled.

Outrageous debt abounds, all future generations with it now are bridled,

While all America waits with anticipation for the next "American Idol."

Disasters strike with debilitating fury and there is little warning.
Around the world devastation reigns, while new havoc nature's forming.
Science plays with nature attempting to create a human clone,
While all America fights with fury to get the newest iPhone.

Protests turning into revolution are cropping up across the land;
A people of great confusion, a mob steadily growing out of hand.
Government intrusion continually increasing, there remains no safe bastion,
While all America is gravely concerned with wearing the latest fashion.

The signs foretold of the end of the age are increasing with intensity.
The evil thoughts of all men now grow with a great propensity.
A celestial rider waits for His signal to ride, a trumpet proclaims the end,
While all America diligently seeks for another Facebook friend.

DON'T UPSET THE APPLE CART

"For the time will come when people will not endure sound doctrine, but they will gather to themselves teachers in accordance with their own desires, having itching ears, and they will turn their ears away from the truth and turn to myths." (2 Timothy 4:3-4) All you have to do to find the preachers and teachers who are willing to tickle itching ears is turn on your TV — they are plenty. Cognitive dissonance, unfortunately, thrives in the church house as well as in the world.

DON'T UPSET THE APPLE CART
by Randy Conway
Copyright © 2017

Don't upset the apple cart,

Just say a prayer and follow your heart.

Don't be rude and speak of condemnation,

We teach love and kindness to our congregations.

Don't speak of frightening things that we don't understand,

After all, God is love and we are in His hands.

We think the men who warn are just playing on our fear,

Trying to make a dollar selling us survival gear.

We're confused by terms like Singularity;

We want another message on Prosperity.

Some are talking about something called Transhuman;

That's not for church; it causes way too much confusion.

Fallen angels, stargates and giants are the subjects of fairy tales.
We're even in doubt about the account of Jonah and the whale.
Spirits and demons should stay up on the movie screen;
We don't need to hear that scary stuff about a Black Awakening.

Conspiracy theories are fine if you're watching the cable news,
But in the church house we should leave out any political views.
And all this talk about the Pope; isn't he a man of God?
I think this story of the Pope and aliens is just a little odd.

Men are trying to scare us in regard to the economy.
Doesn't God give to us some kind of economic autonomy;
Especially when we put a little of our money in the offering?
Besides, men still buy stocks and bonds and some are profiting.

We shouldn't scare our parishioners with talk of war;
Not since Pearl Harbor has there been a battle on our shores.
We are insulated in our beliefs knowing that God is love
And we think He sends us peace on the wings of doves.

WOE to the foolish who wish to silence the Watchmen.

God IS love but there is more to the Biblical regimen.

Let those with ears hear while the Spirit still strives;

Fools are taken unaware and they will not survive.

Those who hear the Word and accept the Truth will be ready
for tomorrow;

The foolish in their "normalcy bias" will have to face their
sorrow.

Sorrow for the times they have ignored when God sent
warnings;

The bliss they found in ignorance will in a twinkling be turned
to mourning.

The enemy is upon us and many are already deceived.

Jesus is knocking at the door and waiting to receive

All who will heed the call and in repentance turn to Him.

Those who are uncomfortable with Truth will find the future
grim.

FAITH FALLING TO PIECES

This poem is inspired from the book of Amos; a must read. Because it is the work of one of the minor prophets, it is sometimes overlooked; however, it's not only a book of prophecy, but a clear word regarding judgment for sin and blessing for righteousness. "...though you have built houses of hewn stone, you will not dwell in them; though you have planted pleasant vineyards, you will not drink their wine." (Amos 5:11) "Seek good and not evil, so that you may live..." (Amos 5:14a)

FAITH FALLING TO PIECES
by Randy Conway
Copyright © 2017

The man who tells the truth is now despised;

His words are called conspiracy, the masses think them lies.

We have turned justice into bitterness, saying good is evil;

Leaders proclaiming evil is now good, stupid arrogant people.

Pretending that the poor are of such great concern,

Yet using them at every chance, abusing at every turn.

Building our cherished mansions made of stone,

But alas, those mansions will never be our home.

Planting vineyards of business in great abundance,

Yet our lips will not know or ever taste its succulence.

The prudent man in court remains quiet in times as these;

In the midst of evil God's mercy is what he pleads.

God has spoken; He will pass through our midst.
He isn't coming to offer us a loving gentle kiss.
He is coming to judge with a fierce and mighty fist;
His searing fire of Judgment we shall not miss.

Take heart in His promise; if we seek Him we will live.
Suffering and blessing, life and death are His to give.
Devoid of hope, our faith will fall to pieces;
Peace comes only to those whose minds are fixed on Jesus.

Do not trust in worldly churches, congregations loving lies;
God sees the people assembled and by Him they are despised.
Our offerings are not accepted and our songs remain unheard;
It is only by true repentance that the heart of God is stirred.

It is time to take down our shrines that glorify our sin,
Shake off our complacency and denial of the state we're in.
He is the hope that rebuilds our weak and shattered faith;
Life is waiting for those who are willing to seek His Face.

FINAL WARNINGS

This poem is one of the oldest works in this collection; one of the first poems I received regarding the Day of the Lord and the "end times." To my own regret in earlier years I didn't date my poetry and exact dates are not in my memory bank; along with a lot of other stuff I don't remember. I do write things down more frequently now to aid in remembering, but then I forget where I put the paper I wrote it on. Nevertheless, I still have the poem and am happy to share it with you. "...for this people's heart has grown dull. Their ears have become hard of hearing, and they have closed their eyes, lest they should see with their eyes and hear with their ears and understand with their hearts, and turn, and I should heal them." (Matthew 13:15) "Jesus answered them, Take heed that no one deceives you. For many will come in My name, saying, 'I am the Christ,' and will deceive many. You will hear of wars and rumors of war. See that you are not troubled. For all these things must happen, but the end is not yet." (Matthew 24:4-6)

FINAL WARNINGS
by Randy Conway
Copyright © 2017

The annals of our history were written before events took place,

Given to the pens of prophets through the void of time and space;

Telling of the things to come and the future of the human race,

Preparation for the Bride of Christ and things that we must face.

How is it then that we don't know? Are we too blind to see
The birth pains of the things to come, the entrance to eternity?
Is the written Word considered useless scribble of antiquity,
While events unfold around us, proving the written
prophecies?

All of nature now is churning, wrestling with the labor pains;
Birthing disaster heaped on man until our hope is drained.
But we are told these things must come and we are not to be
alarmed;
False prophets spew their lies from hell while all the world is
charmed.

Wars to avenge war to justify another, while rumors tell of
more.
The earth will shake, the seas will stir, the wind rise up and
roar.
Those who claim the Name of God will suffer by evil's hand;
The weak will fall and shrink away, but the faithful true will
stand.

Repentance is our preparation for the days ahead;

Turn from our sin and degradation, be by the Spirit led.

The hearts of men now full of sin as they were before the flood;

They ignored the message of the Rain and we ignore the Blood.

The Blood of Christ shed for all mankind;

The blood of martyrs crying out through time.

The message has now been told to every single nation

And we scoff in arrogance denying our own emancipation.

Sin is no longer creeping to steal the hearts of men;

Already hearts are stone and deprivation rules the land.

We have sold our souls for every temporal pleasure,

Ever increasing wickedness, forfeiting all future treasure.

Let those who read or hear these words fully understand

A Day is coming very soon when the stars will fall to land.

The sun and moon will give no light, that Day is soon at hand

And these are the signs long foretold of the coming Son of Man.

The call is clear, turn back to God, seek His mercy and His
Grace;
Confessing our sin while we turn to Him, falling on our face
Before the Son of God at Calvary, where Jesus took our place.
We must choose whom we believe and what we will embrace.

The truth foretold or Satan's lies, the choice is ours to make.
The time is short, the game is done and they perish who
hesitate.
The watchman on the wall is loudly sounding out the warning;
The night is now upon us and tomorrow brings the mourning.

Only those who know Him not need to fear this cry;
The Blood-bought child rejoices for redemption's drawing
nigh.
The layers of time and space will tear away, revealing heavens
shore
And all creation in exultation will see the Lord of Lords!

HAVE YOU PRAYED?

J. Vernon McGee, a well-known pastor, always spoke of prayer changing things and the fact that God remains in control. "There will be signs in the sun and the moon and the stars; and on the earth distress of nations, with perplexity, the sea and the waves roaring; men fainting from fear and expectation of what is coming on the inhabited earth. For the powers of heaven will be shaken." (Luke 21:25-26) "The effective fervent prayer of a righteous man accomplishes much." (James 5:16b) We are called to be patient and establish our hearts, for the coming of the Lord is drawing near.

HAVE YOU PRAYED?
by Randy Conway
Copyright © 2017

The words of warning by true Watchmen are being continually shared,

Though some accuse them of nefarious intentions their words are not to scare.

From a heart of genuine concern they warn so that people might be prepared

And every day it seems we see the evidence of things that were declared.

Christian, take to your knees and fervidly proclaim repentance;

Fall on your knees before the Lord and not just for your deliverance

From things that lie in the future; the things that will cause
men's hearts to fail;
But pray that men will turn to God and see through the
delusional veil.

My heart is heavy when I think of what will become of those I
know and love.
What pain will they endure and who will survive when this
push has become shove?
Pray for open eyes and pray for open ears; pray for the very
young and pray also for the old.
When the money is gone and the electric bill is due, many will
be overcome by bitter cold.

Hunger I think would be a most slow and miserable way to
die;
The despair and broken hearts of mothers as they listen to their
children cry.
Pray also for the Remnant, for persecution is not to come, it
has arrived.
If you're not fervently praying then perhaps you too are living
in the lie.

The lie that says the words of warning are nothing more than the prose of fools;
Those who believe this lie will fit nicely into the New World Order rule.
Have you considered how many homeless people there will be in the days ahead,
Or do thoughts of your favorite team winning fill your mind instead?

EMP's or Nuclear War will leave families, lives and nations wounded;
When riots hit the streets, stores, families and lives are going to be looted.
How much pain will be incurred so the transhumanists can play their games?
Have you prayed for anyone's protection from the chemical spray that rains?

What of giants? Do you believe that fairy tales are their only home?
Perhaps we should be deep in prayer before the giants again do roam.
Should we not pray for that power which overcomes all the power of the enemy?

The future is held only by the Living God, not some imagined immunity.

I will pray for those I love, for those that I hold dear,
For a day is fast approaching when men's hearts will fail for fear.
I pray for those I've never met, that all will be awakened
To looking after those things which are coming on the earth:
"for the powers of heaven shall be shaken."

HERE AND NOW OR YET TO COME?

This poem comes from the 3rd and 4th chapters of 2ⁿᵈ Timothy, but I will restrain from sharing the entire passage here. You can read the book for yourself. It is a quick read, as it is only four chapters long, and it gives pertinent insight into what is prophesied and expected as we move with continuing greater velocity into the last days. "Know this: In the last days perilous times will come. Men will be lovers of themselves, lovers of money, boastful, proud, blasphemers, disobedient to parents, unthankful, unholy, without natural affection, truce-breakers, slanderers, unrestrained, fierce, despisers of those who are good, traitors, reckless, conceited, lovers of pleasures more than lovers of God, having a form of godliness, but denying its power..." (2 Timothy 3:1-5)

HERE AND NOW OR YET TO COME?
by Randy Conway
Copyright © 2017

Love is not lost nor is love suffering poor health;

Love has just been perverted so that men now love only self.

But of course love is not reserved only for one's self,

Love is clearly abundant when you consider man's love of wealth.

The days ahead, so it is said, will be difficult, dangerous, painful and perilous.

We must be prepared for savage times that will become most grievous.

Men will become headstrong and haughty, forsaking any self-control;
Unthankful, unloving, unholy, unforgiving–that will be man's role.

Are these merely warnings of days to come or have these days arrived?
The learned men increase in knowledge while clinging to their lies.
Acknowledging the possibility of a god or some form of higher power,
But still denying that there is a Mighty God with all-consuming power.

Comparing what is said to come with what is here today
Is a frightening revelation of what the Scriptures say.
Loving pleasure, a world of traitors, brutal men despising what is good;
They would destroy any man who interferes with them if they only could.

All these words were warnings to a young man long ago,
Telling him that evil men will deceive both young and old;

And those who desire to live a godly life will suffer for their faith.

We must then become equipped, for the days to come will not be safe.

Are these words warnings of things the future will provide,
Or a revealing to those who see that the future has arrived?
Those who have ears must hear, and those with eyes must see
The "way of the world" is Scripture fulfilled, not just an anomaly.

I CALLED YOU BUT YOU DID NOT ANSWER

This poem is convicting and a little scary to me. It's truly a description of cause and effect and I must ask myself, "Am I listening?" Over and over the ancient Scriptures remind us that those with ears should hear what the Spirit says. "But you are those who forsake the LORD, who forget My holy mountain, who prepare a table for Fortune, and who furnish the drink offering for Destiny. I will destine you for the sword, and you all shall bow down to the slaughter; because when I called, you did not answer; when I spoke, you did not hear but did evil before My eyes and chose that in which I did not delight." (Isaiah 65:11-12) "...I said, 'Here I am, here I am'..." (Isaiah 65:1)

I CALLED YOU BUT YOU DID NOT ANSWER
by Randy Conway
Copyright © 2017

Another tempest is blowing!

Is there no one to send a warning?

Disaster sings another refrain;

We are left naked, lying in shame.

I called you but you did not answer.

I spoke but you did not listen.

The threat of war and people live in fear,

Is there no one left to proclaim that peace is near?

The threat of extinction hovers over the children,

Is there no champion found among the sons of men?

I called you but you did not answer.
I spoke but you did not listen.

Has famine become our lot; hunger our only hope?
The bellies ache and men are crazed, we wonder how we'll
cope.
Poverty like an aggressive cancer has now come upon us.
Is there no king, no president, no leader we can trust?

I called you but you did not answer.
I spoke but you did not listen.

Where are the men who in Truth cried out?
Why are church doors locked, what has come about?
Where are those who filled our ears with promises?
Why are there no prayers, no pulpits, no armistice?

I called you but you did not answer.
I spoke but you did not listen.
All day long I have held out My hands.
Let him who has an ear hear the Voice of the Lord calling,
"Here am I, Here am I."

I WEEP FOR THE UNPREPARED

Thinking about the "prepper" movement and having a keen interest in biblical prophecy, I noticed a couple of things. First, there are many scoffers who deride those who attempt to prepare, and eviscerate the watchmen who are warning people to prepare. The second thing I noticed is that this leaves many people in a quandary as to whether they should prepare or not. I also thought about those who want to make future preparations but their financial positions won't allow them to. And then there are those who could, but refuse. It is a sad predicament for all. But to those who are stressed by this whole "prepper" movement, I would give this word: it doesn't take money to prepare your heart, and preparing the heart is the ultimate preparation. "Therefore God will send them a strong delusion, that they will believe the lie…" (2 Thessalonians 2:11)

I WEEP FOR THE UNPREPARED
by Randy Conway
Copyright © 2017

I weep for those who are caught unaware,

When men will die and it's too late for prayer.

How sad that many will not believe

And the wages of their denial they will receive.

When judgment falls the people will be frantic,

The children will cry and the mothers will be in a panic.

The fathers will watch their loved ones suffer

Because they were too proud to establish a buffer.

The buffer is not that you can escape from the storm,
But to do what you can to keep your family fed and keep them warm.
A prudent man foresees evil and takes action to save himself;
How sad to be a father who refused to even put some food up on a shelf.

The tears will flow along with rivers of blood,
Both mingling in the streets, a cruel and bitter flood.
Money will be changed and who knows what will be its worth.
Now is the time to hear, not when trouble has been birthed.

I weep for the women and I weep for the children,
I pray for protection from Satan's employed villains.
But alas I can but pray, I cannot act for you.
You must decide for yourself that the Word of God is true.

Your decision will affect today, tomorrow and forever.
The heavenly Father weeps for He has invited whomsoever.
Those who refuse to believe the truth as the watchmen cry
Are accursed then with a delusion, that they should believe the lies.

I weep for those who will be caught in the terrible panic.

How can you describe what is coming except to say it will be satanic?

Grievous times that God has warned us about;

Multitudes scoff the warnings, living in this world of spiritual drought.

Salvation waits for those who will be saved;

Those who reject Jesus are destined to be enslaved.

The enemy of our souls has planned for you a future that is depraved.

In the palm of the Father's hand the believer's name has been engraved.

ONWARD CHRISTIAN SOLDIERS

This poem is one of my personal favorites because the call to "armor up," or, as author, columnist, radio host and my friend, Doug Hagmann (Hagmann and Hagmann Report) puts it, "Saddle for battle," remains as relevant and contemporary today as it did when the Apostle Paul wrote his letter to the first century church at Ephesus. Based on Ephesians chapter 6 and on the promise of the coming King of Kings, it is a call to be ready in all seasons. But readers beware: if you draw that line in the sand and put on the whole armor of God you WILL encounter a fight. The enemy of our souls does not ignore the Christian Soldier. "Finally, my brothers, be strong in the Lord and in the power of His might. Put on the whole armor of God that you may be able to stand against the schemes of the devil." (Ephesians 6:10-11)

ONWARD CHRISTIAN SOLDIERS
by Randy Conway
Copyright © 2017

Satan's army stands full force and hurls their fiery darts;

With legion upon legion they're aiming for your heart.

So few who know we've been supplied with armor and a sword,

And that the victory is ours when Jesus Christ is Lord.

If it seems at times the enemy has the upper hand,

It's because we shine our armor and we fail to take a stand.

There's no time to stand at ease, we must be always ready for the fight,

So I don my armor now to be a soldier of the Light.

On the day when heaven's army comes with flaming swords of fire,
The final battle will be won and chains will bind the liar.
The heavens will resound as hooves beat against the sky
And the saints and angels will descend from their camp on high.

On that day I hope I'm found with armor not shining bright,
But rather shows the signs and scars of being in the fight.
So Christian heed the call today, be a soldier of the cross,
For every battle won today is truly Satan's loss.

As soldiers we must remain prepared, for we don't battle flesh and blood,
But principalities and powers in a dark and raging flood.

RUN FOR YOUR LIFE

For a few years now many public figures have spoken of expatriating, or building a "safe place" to run to — a "bug-out" location. There are companies that have developed and sold "Bug-out Bags" in the event that you have to make a run for it. It was in thinking about the need to bug-out that brought the thoughts penned in this poem. My wife tells me it scares her, but I remind her of that which she knows; God is our hope, our rock, our shelter and our salvation and we only have to run to Him and He is not far off. (She knows the Scriptures better than I do.) "...but those who wait upon the LORD shall renew their strength; they shall mount up with wings as eagles, they shall run and not be weary, and they shall walk and not faint." (Isaiah 40:31) The narrow gate, which is the one Jesus tells us to enter through, is described in Matthew 7:13-14, while the wide gate that the man of the world would choose for himself is described in Proverbs 14:12. Jeremiah 29:11 details the plans that God has for His children.

RUN FOR YOUR LIFE
by Randy Conway
Copyright © 2017

Are you ready to run; will your legs have the strength if you have to flee?

Will your lungs have the capacity so that when running you can breathe?

Where will you go if you feel you must run?

Can you carry your daughter; can you carry your son?

Some will run for safety when the earth is violently shaking;
Some will run in fear as ominous storms are in the making.
Some will run to the store to gather food and some supplies,
Finding empty shelves they will run until they die.

They will run across the land, some will head across the seas;
They will run into the mountains, they will run from a disease.
They will run from searing heat, they will run from bitter cold;
Many runners will succumb to death whether they be young or
they be old.

They will run to the bank to check on their accounts;
They will run into a panic when they see their balance amount.
Like a chicken without a head there'll be no compass to their
running;
Fear will cause men's hearts to fail for the things that will be
coming.

Across the earth men will run both to and fro.
Some will run to family, others to friends they know.
Some will run to authorities believing they will surely rescue
them,
And the rulers of this world will stand with open arms,
feigning to be a friend.

Are you prepared to run; do you have the strength?

Can you run for days or miles? Can you run great lengths?

Most will run a broad and easy path that leads only to destruction.

For all of time men have run this path led by a great seduction.

A remnant will find a path quite narrow; it is a path that's straight.

They won't need to run in fear or leave their future up to fate;

They know they only need to run as far as the cross of Calvary.

Jesus is waiting there and in His arms they have placed their destiny.

There are evil plans and disasters coming to this age;

Death is coming like a storm in order to collect sin's wage.

Many will run; they will run for their life,

But their running will be in vain unless they run to Jesus Christ.

For the believer with faith who reads the words that the prophets penned,

They will know God's thoughts toward us; "thoughts of peace, and not of evil, to give you an expected end."

SOMETHING IMPENDING

Shadow Government, Deep State, Elite Rulers, Banksters and the fact that all wars are bankers wars are topics that have been hidden or ridiculed when exposed. Furthermore, the favorite way to discount truth is to just call it "conspiracy theory." Now you can add "fake news," and any legitimacy is immediately gone as the "sheeple" continue on. Nearly every one you talk to will agree that things are different than they have ever been and most feel a sense of urgency or at least a sense of something's not quite right.
Here's the good news: you don't have to be concerned about following all the right guidelines and lists for preparation, or discovering exactly how to decipher fact from fiction. Be concerned about following the Living God and "Lean not on your own understanding but in all your ways acknowledge Him and He will direct you in all your ways." (Proverbs 3:5-8) To the believer, don't let the following poem discourage you or worry you. If you are not a follower of Jesus Christ, you should be very concerned about the following poem's warning.

SOMETHING IMPENDING
by Randy Conway
Copyright © 2017

There's a sense of uncertainty that's churning in my spirit.

There's an agitation in the earth, at times I think I hear it.

There's a seething among the people, I wonder should we fear it?

Something is on our horizon; I believe we are very near it.

It's like that feeling you have when you think you're being watched;

An uneasiness that you think would be better left unsought.
The hair stands up on the back of your neck without
substantial reason
And it's growing without restraint like an unwanted cancerous
lesion.

Do evil men make evil plans? Are there any happenstances?
Or are conditions manipulated creating blueprinted
circumstances?
When a crisis comes, men act according to their fear;
Their emotions rule and to their values they may not adhere.

Are there powers who realize this phenomenon?
Could it be this Hegelian dialectic reaction is what their
counting on?
Frustration describes my ability at explanation.
Those who listen accuse me of flirting with sensation.

The more expository I become in attempting to explain,
The more those who listen think surely he's not sane.
Let those who have an ear hear the word that does not falter;
The deaf, in their delusion, the message have not altered.

The Day of the Lord will surely come just as God described;
A day of judgment where evil men will have no place to hide.
The events that are coming to this world are just a preparation
For the coming of the King of Kings, it is a time of
anticipation.

We have not been given a spirit of fear but a mind that's
sound;
We will endure the days ahead if we stand on higher ground.
Those whose hearts remain cold and cling tightly to confusion
Will fall faint and die–the result of holding to a great delusion.

War lies at our borders; death waits at our door.
Economic failure seems more prevalent than ever before.
Famine is rapidly advancing spreading shore to shore.
Disaster is brewing above and below as never known in yore.

Disease is hungry and waiting to be released.
Men will cry for death to come in order to find relief.
It is time for men with eyes that see to look into the sky,
For when this travail is upon the earth our redemption is
drawing nigh.

THE DARK FRONTIER

Electro Magnetic Pulse (or EMP), financial crises, New World Order and WW3 seem to be things we hear about on a daily basis. If all of the events described in this short poem were to come upon on us all at once, the world as we know it and our lives would never be the same again. There was a time when the "nuclear threat" was the biggest thing we had to be concerned with (Remember duck and cover? What a joke!) Now, we have a plethora of impending threats to deal with and we surely are upon a precipice or the very edge of a dark frontier. The truth of these threats is always filtered through the mesh of political correctness before it reaches the people, so that the people can be maintained in the lemming mind set. But I have good news: "The people who walked in darkness have seen a great light; those who dwell in the land of the shadow of death, (that's us) upon them the light has shined." (Isaiah 9:2) And one day the government will be on His shoulders, and all this threat will be no more. On that day, the kingdoms of the world will have become the kingdoms of our Lord and His Christ! (Revelation 11:15)

THE DARK FRONTIER
by Randy Conway
Copyright © 2017

Threatening, the always foreboding "EMP" seems daily

imminently to appear;

We sit silently apathetic, waiting at the precipice of a Dark

Frontier.

Men are unwilling or too afraid to act, afraid to speak; the truth

is feared,

The tolerance of the people bears a price, costing all that we hold dear.

The threat of a global monetary reset is continually ignored while riches are revered;
Facing the threat of financial ruin, we have arrived at the dawn of a Dark Frontier.
Men holding onto earthly treasures with an iron grip; others holding on just to persevere.
Regardless of social position the strength of their grip is fueled by a growing fear.

Our reality is that all government's play the people as pawns in their game of social engineers,
As a New World Order encroaches moving us continually closer to an unknown Dark Frontier.
Trusting elected officials, trusting our ignorance, believing A New World Order is nothing queer;
Trusting the talking heads spewing lies from hell, telling the masses what they would have us hear.

The threat of war is at our door, everywhere the sound of marching draws ever near;

Public servants militarized, drones fly in the public square,
signs of the coming Dark Frontier.

All warnings, all truth, all light is quickly crushed lest the
sleeping masses hear;

Still a faithful few remain vigilant in proclaiming Truth, listen
those with ears.

Men playing with the weather, experiments with sound, skies
filled with poison raining down like tears,

Conspiracy is the lie that turns men's heads away, calling truth
conspiracy to hide the Dark Frontier.

Science playing with our DNA, longing to be immortal,
pretending they are gods they will have no peers.

The Scriptures foretold these days would come; the darkness is
now sharpened, piercing like a spear.

The darkness is more than just the absence of any light; it
consumes all men and minds are seared.

Darkness bearing the fears of night, this will be our existence
in the New World Dark Frontier.

Darkness flourishes, and then feeds the black hearts of men
whose love of sin is hellishly sincere.

But hope is not lost and not every future dark; Jesus Christ the
Light has promised He is here.

We cannot see what lies ahead but the condition of our hearts determines our future years;

Our choices will determine our tomorrow; we can choose hope or succumb to the Dark Frontier.

We can choose to prepare or we can ignore; we can repent or we can continue darkness to revere.

Jesus made a way through His Blood at Calvary; the future is yours to make, the choices are very clear.

Enter into the Light or enter the Dark Frontier.

THE EDGE OF ETERNITY

First Peter 5:8 says, "Be sober and watchful, because your adversary the devil walks around as a roaring lion, seeking whom he may devour." And we have forgotten or ignored the words of James in the book of the Bible that bears his name, chapter 4, verses 7 & 8, "Therefore submit yourselves to God. Resist the devil, and he will flee from you. Draw near to God and He will draw near to you." We are on the edge of eternity; life is not guaranteed, but death is. The Bible says it is appointed unto man once to die. We all have an appointment; we just don't know the day, the hour or even the location, but death will find us at the appointed time. The number of our days is likened to a vapor or mist that is here for a moment and then gone. As of this writing, it has been three days since I attended the funeral of my own mother. Just hours ago before writing this paragraph, my sister called to inform me that her mother-in-law just passed away. As individuals and as a nation we quickly forget the frailty of life and the closeness of the end of our lives and the end of this age. "Look, now is the accepted time; look, now is the day of salvation." (2 Corinthians 6:2b)

THE EDGE OF ETERNITY
by Randy Conway
Copyright © 2017

Satan, like a lion, still roams throughout the earth,

Seeking whom he may devour. Has he found a home within the church?

Let those with ears hear the Spirit calling out for

Righteousness.

Sadly we have embraced the world and dearly love our impiousness.

God's call remains insistent, yet to evil we offer no resistance,
And Satan doesn't have to flee for we have abandoned falling to our knees.
It has come that our time has all been spent;
Today is the Day of Salvation, today we must repent.

When Jesus shed His Blood, crucified on Calvary,
It wasn't a religious ceremony or to prove His piety.
It was the ultimate sacrifice; He was trading life for life,
Yet we reject the sacrifice, holding tightly to our vice.

We are racing with rapidity ever quickly towards eternity,
While Salvation slips not through our fingers, but our knees.
The Watchman continues warning of coming evil and calamity,
And the warnings are scoffed as conspiracy; just gibberish of insanity.

The roaring lion is prowling at our window; he is lurking at our door.

The Watchmen warn, the Spirit calls, destruction awaits if we ignore.

Today is the Day of Salvation; this is the Day for Deliverance;

We are anxious over the unknown, yet deaf to the call for repentance.

We know not what lies beyond the dawn or what evil prowls the night;

The unknown enslaves us to fear, for the unknown we cannot fight.

We don't need to know what tomorrow holds, only who holds tomorrow.

Repentance is our preparation to enter the unknown, but refusal leads to sorrow.

Fear will flee when we're on our knees;

Salvation waits for all mankind at Calvary.

We pray Lord open our eyes that we might clearly see;

We exist now on the very edge of our eternity.

THE GREAT DAY OF THE LORD AND HIS CHASTENING ROD

Sometime late in the 7th century B.C., the prophet Zephaniah spoke of the "Day of the Lord." In fact, Zephaniah uses this term more than any other prophet. He refers to the dreadful and fearsome consequences of the coming "Day of the Lord." But, he doesn't leave the recipients of his message with just the dread of this day; he brings also a message of hope and restoration by telling us that escape from this awful day is possible, but conditional upon returning to the Lord. Judgment comes to those nations (or people) who reject the Lord, but for those who belong to God, we are told that God himself will sing over them. I would rather hear His singing than hear His judgment. According to Zephaniah, chapter 1, the Great Day of the Lord "will utterly consume all things on the face of the earth."

THE GREAT DAY OF THE LORD AND HIS CHASTENING ROD
by Randy Conway
Copyright © 2017

Keep silent and listen so that you may hear

The warning proclaiming the Day of the Lord is near.

God with outstretched arm will sweep across the land

And death will follow every movement of His hand.

Those who trust in their silly superstitions,

Those who know not God but only their religion

Will hear the cries and cover their ears from the wailing,

For the crash in the hills is the sound of Heaven assailing.

The Day of the Lord is coming quickly, it is very near.
Listen to the cry, it comes with bitter tears.
The shouting of the Warrior will pierce unto the sky;
It is a day of trumpets sounding, a day of battle cry.

That Day will be a day of anguish and a day of wrath;
A day filled with distress with trouble at our backs.
Blackness and darkness, clouds and gloom;
In the fire of His jealousy the world will be consumed.

Silver will be worthless and gold will be the same.
This Day is coming because the people have profaned
His name, the Almighty God, and have not revered the Lord.
It is our sin and depravation that have brought today this
sword.

Gather together, gather together all you nations;
Before it's too late we must make reparations.
Seek the Lord all you humble in the land;
Seek the Lord all who do what He commands.

We must seek humility and righteousness;
Seek it now before our time has all egressed.
If we humble ourselves before Almighty God,
We can be spared this Chastening Rod.

THE RIDERS OF THE APOCALYPSE

One Sunday morning as my wife, Robin, and I were preparing to leave for church, the words to this poem came rushing into my head. It was literally time to leave when I sat down at the computer and began typing the following verses. Now, I am not a typist. In fact, I never took a typing class of any kind. I couldn't tell you how many words per minute I was typing, but my wife just stood there watching in amazement. It was truly an agent of the Lord moving my hands across the keys. Within just a very few minutes (I couldn't tell you the exact amount of time), this poem was typed and printed and I took it to church where I shared it during the worship time. I've received nearly all of my poems by hearing the words roll through my head (usually in the middle of the night), but have never had another experience quite like the morning I received this poem. It is based on the opening of the "seals" as recorded in the 6th chapter of the book of Revelation.

THE RIDERS OF THE APOCALYPSE
by Randy Conway
Copyright © 2017

There was a time when in the quiet of the night:

A distant sound of horses, I thought that I could hear

Riders on the clouds continually drawing near.

No longer reserved for the quiet is the sound ringing in my ear;

I feel the vibration of their hooves because the Riders they are

here.

One of the Riders has set his course,

He has pulled the reigns and has turned his horse.

The prints of hooves mark the sky and the land,

He rides with a Bow held tight in his hand.

Those in the path of this White horse will fall

To their demise for ignoring God's call.

He is bent upon man's defeat

And nations soon will lie at his feet.

No longer do I only hear, but now I see

A Red horse with a Rider mounted on this steed.

The Sword he wields strikes the minds of men

And a hate-filled delusion has consumed every one of them.

A ubiquitous blackness fills the sky for a Rider on a Black
horse has arrived.

He weighs the gold with Scales which he holds high.

Now money has no value, soon even bread it will not buy;

In a shelter beneath a bridge I can hear the hungry cry.

A fourth horseman rides and the whole earth turns pale.

Death comes with many faces; a pandemic races while
medicine fails.

The excruciating pains of hunger haunt the bellies of the children.
The crows take flight to eat the dead; they feast in flocks of millions.

The Pale horseman is riding hard and Death and Hell are on his heels.
When he arrives there is no escape and the entire earth will feel
The fury of demons, evil reptilians and the death that Hades seeks.
A fourth of mankind will fall as he rides, both the strong and the weak.

He rides not alone but he has unleashed
The bear, the lion and other beasts.
Man for refuge will diligently seek,
But man is now the wild one's feast.

The whole earth soon will violently quake,
The sun will turn black, the face of wraith.
Blood fills the moon that hangs in the night,
Stars fall from the heavens unable to sustain their flight.

But soon the heavens will rip open for all to see

Yet another Rider mounted on His steed.

On a White horse he comes to judge and to make war;

A Sword like lighting from his mouth will swiftly soar.

All the armies of Heaven will ride with Him,

Striking down the nations who covenant with sin.

He will rule them with an Iron Scepter

And the evil ruler He has intercepted.

When the horsemen have completed their ride

A wondrous thing is prophesied.

The Kingdoms of this world will become the Kingdoms of our Lord,

They will be the Kingdoms of His Christ, and all heaven worships God in one accord.

Jesus Christ will tread out the winepress of the wrath of God.

God will be shown to the world even as He is shown through Gog.

And on that Day all of man, even Satan and all of Satan's hordes

Will bow their knees before the King of Kings and Lord of Lords.

On that Day it will be too late to make your choice.

Today is the Day of Salvation; listen now to the Watchman's voice.

There will be no surviving the days ahead by any natural means;

Your future is dependent upon your repentance and the grace of the coming King.

THE "TRANS" AND THE "TECH"

There may be some terms in this poem that are not familiar to everyone, but don't be dismayed; I have included a glossary of terms in order to make sure that they are understood. Included in these verses you will find many of today's conspiracy facts–not theories–along with their origins from the "watchers" referred to in the book of Enoch, who are the ben-Elohim seen in Genesis chapter 6. The Prophet Jeremiah, in chapter 25, speaks of a "noise," or in some versions a "tumult," that will be heard even in the remotest parts of the earth. This noise will be heard because the Lord has a controversy with the nations and He will bring charges against them. In fact, He is bringing judgment upon all flesh. Those judged to be wicked, according to the Bible, will be put to the sword.

THE "TRANS" AND THE "TECH"
by Randy Conway
Copyright © 2017

Around the world people can feel the rumble and hear the

sounds,

As CERN beats against the gates of hell to free the giants from

the ground.

As the Collider continually increases the TEV, against the

portals they continually pound,

And as the noises perplex the masses, I am wondering what is

it they have found.

Tech-tattoos and bio-locks on phones,

Smart TVs so "they" can watch us in our homes.

My credit card has an implanted chip;

Who are the technocrats that want us in their grip?

Transhuman, Transgender, Transgovernment, Translife;

The agenda to alter humanity is growing increasingly rife.

Genetic engineering to alter the seed of man so we will be Transhuman,

Began long ago when the age of the world was still Antediluvian.

To change and alter what is a man, is an ancient dark and practiced plan.

It started before the fallen ones bred with man, which by God was expressly banned.

When deep in Eden Eve fell to temptation and with Satan she agreed,

Then was born the enmity which still exists between the seed.

Genetic mutations followed the fallen when dimensional portals were crossed.

Abominations flourished as war raged against Pure Seed; it was a genetic holocaust.

The Creator God had His fill of this Transhuman plague and the corruption of the blood.
To remove the plague destroying man and seed, God sent a worldwide cleansing flood.

What are the goals behind today's technology and the desire to alter our genetics?
What is a man if not body, spirit and soul? The coming mutation would be synthetic.
Will this science give us gods or giants? Will this "science of deity resurrection" deliver our demise?
And what of the machines being built to learn? What becomes of man when machines begin to rise?

If God would not tolerate the earlier attempts to mutate his creation,
Then it is a fool who believes He will tolerate our present day mutations.
God's coming judgment will be fast and fierce and harsh;
"Trans" is the transition changing this age into an apocalyptic march.

Today's fallen angel technology comes with an enormous price;

It will be like Eve's unholy curiosity which produced a painful sacrifice.

The goals for Transhumanism and fallen angels seem very much the same;

And now, just as then, to counter God's perfect plan will only result in pain.

Can we survive gene editing or the coaptation of man and machine?

Will the splicing of technology and human DNA bring a new regime?

GRIN technology, the JASONS and Illuminists desiring a new Atlantis,

Spouting all the benefits and "heaven scenarios" in order to enchant us.

Was not Nimrod enchanted with the gateway to God and became a gibborim?

Are we not enchanted with the gateway to God as CERN plays with particle beams?

Was the world not flooded in ages past and did not the tower of Babel fall?

Can man pretend to be greater than God with no fear of what will then befall?

Will not a great whirlwind from the coasts of the earth be raised?

God will judge the inhabitants of earth as He has done in former days.

The peaceable habitations are cut down because of the Lord's fierce anger;

In such storms of Judgment Jesus is our only salvation; He is the only anchor.

Glossary for: THE "TRANS" AND THE "TECH"

GRIN technology–Genetics, robotics, artificial intelligence, nanotechnology.

JASONS–JASON Advisory Group, an independent organization of scientists that advise the U.S. government in matters regarding science and technology.

CERN–Referring to the LHC particle collider in Switzerland.

GIBBORIM–A "Mighty Man," Nimrod began to become a gibborim, like the offspring of the fallen angels referred to in Genesis 6:4.

TEV–A unit of energy.

ANTEDILUVIAN–Referring to very old–in biblical use it refers to before the flood.

"Science of deity resurrection" – A portion of the Chapter Title of Chapter 8 of the book, "Zenith 2016," by Thomas Horn.

THE TRUTH IS OUT THERE

One evening, as I was sitting on my couch listening to the Hagmann and Hagmann Report, I noticed all of the reading materials my wife and I had scattered around us. I started jotting down some thoughts for fun. (I believe that Steve Quayle and David Langford may have been guests on the program that evening.) This poem reveals how knowledge of the things of God is increasing and how blessed we are to have at our fingertips so much great information and instruction. After writing the first few lines, I obtained additional reading material and felt compelled to add them as well. I've provided footnotes to bring clarity as to where the information came from. I pray you enjoy it and I also pray that you will take advantage of the wisdom that God has provided through so many great writers and ministers while these works and programs are still available to us. I believe there is coming a day, not too far away, when such resources will be censored.

THE TRUTH IS OUT THERE
by Randy Conway
Copyright © 2017

Angel Wars and portal doors and corrupted DNA,

Giant bones, fairies, gnomes and little sprites at play.

An alien fleet and the power elite and a threat of economic storms;

From *Earth's Earliest Ages* to modern day sages many have worked to warn.

True Legends, anomalies in the heavens and the threat of *Blood on the Altar,*

79

Xenogenesis, an ISIS nemesis and too much of the church has faltered.

The Temple at the Center of Time, orbs that turn on a dime and who is *Petrus Romanus*?

Following the Nephilim, making monsters out of men, what is come upon us?

Forbidden Secrets of the Labyrinth, the truth revealed from Genesis 6; find it in the *Holy Bible*.

A Cosmic Conspiracy, *A Black Awakening* piracy and zombies becoming tribal;

A mystery called *Shemitah*, an endless intifada and *Apollyon is Rising*;

There are *Little Creatures*, secrets in the movie features and New Age visualizing.

To those who will hear the *Weekend Vigilante* shouting,

To those who would know a *Reversing of Hermon* is sprouting,

There are PSYOP deceptions, *The Great Inception*

And the *Shinar Directive* can be seen by those with perception.

A *Caravan to Midnight* carrying information is traveling nigh,

A *Hawk* soars above screeching a message flying high.

Men wonder *Why God Really Exists* and thank God there is still some *Common Sense.*

There is a *Voice of Evangelism* that is direct without riding the fence.

Geo-engineering, vaccination fearing and the masses are being fluoridated;

The Constitution disappearing, secret bio-engineering and Christians being hated.

A health care system that's been hijacked, the threat of asteroid impact; why weren't the people warned?

Watchmen standing on the wall, weary from sounding out the call.

Those who didn't listen, mourn.

References for THE TRUTH IS OUT THERE:
"Angel Wars"–Book by Stephen Quayle, End Time Thunder Publishing
"Earth's Earliest Ages"–Book by George H. Pember, Defender Publishing
"True Legends"–Book by Stephen Quayle, End Time Thunder Publishing
"Blood on the Alter"–Book by Thomas Horn, Defender Publishing
"Xenogenisis"–Book by Stephen Quayle, End Time Thunder Publishing

"Temple at the Center of Time"–Book by David Flynn, Defender Publishing

"Petrus Romanus"–Book by Thomas Horn and Chris Putnam, Defender Publishing

"Forbidden Secrets of the Labyrinth"–Book by Mark Flynn, Defender Publishing

"Cosmic Conspiracy"–Book by Stan Deyo, Deyo Enterprises LLC Publisher

"The Black Awakening"–Book by Russ Dizdar, Preemption Products and Services Publisher

"The Mystery of the Shemitah"–Book by Jonathan Cahn, Frontline Publishers

"Apollyon Rising"–Book by Thomas Horn, Defender Publishing

"Little Creatures"–Book by Stephen Quayle, End Time Thunder Publishing

"Weekend Vigilante"–Radio program and website of Sheila Zylinsky, www.weekendvigilante.com

"Hawk"–Internet Radio Program

"Reversing Hermon"–Book by Dr. Michael Heiser, Defender Publishing

"Great Inception"–Book by Derek Gilbert, Defender Publishing

"Voice of Evangelism"–Ministry of Pastor David Langford

"Shinar Directive"–Book by Dr. Michael Lake, Defender Publishing

"Why God Really Exists"–website of Meranda Devan, www.whygodreallyexists.com

"Caravan to Midnight"–Radio program hosted by John B. Wells

There are some other works that are not named directly but are alluded to and they include:

"Genesis 6 Giants," by Steve Quayle, "The Islamic Antichrist," by Joel Richardson, and Theeconomiccollapse blog.com, by Michael Snyder.

WOULD YOU BELIEVE?

In the Gospel of Matthew, chapter 24, Jesus gives a discourse on the signs of the end of the age. The Gospel of Mark, chapter 13, records the same event and some translations say something at the beginning of this message that I find interesting. One of the disciples tells Jesus to "look" at the magnificent buildings. In Jesus' reply in the Gospel of Mark, verse 5, he begins by saying, "Watch." While we're looking Jesus is telling us to be "watching." The word "watch" carries with it an expectation that the word "look" doesn't. Much like the story of the Prodigal Son, the Father wasn't just "looking" down the road; he was "watching" because he had an expectation. He expected his son to return. The warning is to "Take heed that no one deceives you." (Matthew 24:4 and Mark 13:5) We live in an age of deception. Is anything as it seems?

Would you believe?
Attack on the 2nd Amendment, Banning Bullets, Net Neutrality, American Ministers Jailed for Speaking Truth, Deep Underground Military Bases (DUMBS), False Flags, Secret Prisons, Assassinations, Media Censorship, Re-Defining Who Is A Terrorist, U.S. Abandonment of Allies, Zombie Apocalypse, Climate Change, Forced Vaccinations, FEMA Camps, Fluoride Poisoning, National Debt, Economic Collapse, Incoming Asteroids, Aliens, ISIS, Martial Law, Food Shortage, Climate Manipulation, Earthquakes, Volcanoes, Drought, Foreign Troops on American Soil, NAFTA, Trading with the Enemy Act, Patriot Act, The Secrets of Jekyll Island, Hyper Inflation, Transhumanism, Singularity, Final Pope, One World Religion, New World Order, Nephilim, Fairies, Watchers, CME's, EMP, Nuclear Threat, Ebola, World Wide Strange Sounds, Fukushima Radiation, Common Core, MK Ultra, Black Awakening, Super Bugs, Drones, Uber Surveillance of Citizenry, WWIII, Time Travel, Civil War,

Riots, Militarized Police Forces, Genetic Manipulation, GM Babies, Hedonism, Abortion, Dead Scientists, Dead Bankers, GMO's, Star Gates, Government Cover-ups, Super Storms, Darkness, HAARP, DARPA, Mosquito Robots, Drones, Mass Animal Deaths, Clergy Response Teams, Elite, Illuminati, Reptilians, Parallel Dimensions, Dreams and Visions, Prophecy? Do You Believe The Word of God? WHAT DO YOU BELIEVE?

WOULD YOU BELIEVE?
by Randy Conway
Copyright © 2017

What if I told you everything you thought you knew about the world we live in was in reality a lie?

What if I said the Illuminati is real and there does exist an evil "All Seeing Eye"?

Would you believe the Truth if you encountered Truth face to face?

Would you believe that our every action–yours and mine–are continually being traced?

Would you believe that the condition of our world and nation long ago was planned,

And that a New World Order fashioned by an ancient evil is rapidly besieging man?

Would you believe that technology, in many ways a blessing, is also a curse,

Or that medicine and Pharmacia stopped being about healing
and is about money in the purse?

Would you believe that the Collider experiments taking place
in CERN
Could open unknown portals having consequences of grave
concern?
Or would you rather pop a bag of popcorn and get a movie On
Demand,
Or watch the latest playoff game with the cell phone in your
hand?

Would you believe that the seed of man has been historically
and continually under attack,
Or that the minds of men are manipulated in order to keep
them from fighting back?
What do you believe regarding the world's terrorism threat?
Are you aware that the evening news is nothing more than a
movie set?

If I told you, could you accept that Secret Societies are
manipulating entire nations?
What if I said they have control of religion and the religious
congregations?
Could you accept that our status quo was written long ago,

And true history is now a mystery and the truth we no longer know?

Is there truth behind the old Fairy Tales? Were there giants and are they coming back?
What of the aliens? Are they more than science fiction; are they rather science fact?
What do you believe of prophecy and the days that lie ahead?
Do you think it all conspiracy and only fearful fools build a storehouse for their bread?

The questions regarding what you or I believe are infinite and more than we can name.
Our perception of the Truth does not alter Truth for Truth remains unchanged.
Truth is the same yesterday, today and forever; that is indeed what makes it Truth.
Truth is that for which men desir; for those who are afraid to see, it is an elusive sooth.

One Truth is overwhelming and is realized by precious few,
That God sent His only Son to make a way for me and you.
Your survival through the days ahead will depend upon what you believe;

Would you believe it if I told you God is waiting for you to just receive?

To receive the Free Gift of Life He offers and the promise to see you through.

Through dangers in the days ahead; do you believe fools reject the Gift to their own rue?

It is time for the body of Christ to refrain from being the adulteress,

For the world cannot be drawn unto a church that is found impotent and powerless.

BEFORE THE THUNDER SOUNDS

Chapter 2

A FATHER'S BROKEN HEART

I was inspired to write this poem after pondering the following facts: According to www.theeconomiccollapseblog.com, consumer debt exceeds 12 trillion dollars and the top 25 U.S. banks are holding 222 trillion dollars of exposure to derivatives. The signs of a major economic downturn continue to dominate the financial news. The numbers are continually massaged by the government agencies that post them and the true debt and true unemployment is rarely known or understood by the general population. Many alternative news sites and nearly all conspiracy bloggers reveal what is the hidden–the ultimate plan of FEMA. One only has to look at the laws passed and the executive orders signed that give immeasurable and unprecedented power to FEMA in the event of an emergency or martial law. The government will immediately control all sources of food, water, fuel and transportation. There is also the threat of an attack that would interrupt the continuity of government which would most likely lead to a "Mad Max" world. First John 2:13-18a reads: "I am writing to you, fathers, because you have known Him who is from the beginning. I am writing to you, young men, because you have overcome the evil one. I am writing to you, little children, because you have known the Father. I have written to you, fathers, because you have known Him who is from the beginning. I have written to you, young men, because you are strong, and the word of God lives in you, and you have overcome the evil one. Do not love the world or the things in the world...."

A FATHER'S BROKEN HEART
by Randy Conway
Copyright © 2017

A father's heart is broken as he hears his children cry.

Their mother is near panic in fear that they will die.

"Daddy I am hungry," the children say before they're sent to bed

And the father's barely holding onto sanity from the pounding in his head.

It is not from lack of caring; he works hard every day.

They had a comfortable living and received a decent pay.

Now his wife is blaming him for the pantry being bare

And the fighting is wearing on all of them as their tempers flare.

There is little food that can be bought and his check won't even buy bread.

They both wonder how much longer they'll have a roof above their heads.

Even if he is fortunate enough to continue working, what will it avail?

The entire economy is crumbling, the system now has failed.

He didn't heed the warnings; he thought they were given by
merchants of fear,
And now those things of which they warned are not coming,
they are here.
He thought it silly to make any preparation;
Like many others he thought warnings just to be sensation.

The temperature is getting colder; without power there'll be no
heat,
And in three more days they won't even have a cracker left to
eat.
How can the power be off? He thinks, "I always paid my bill."
His wife must take medicine but the drug store hasn't got her
pills.

Yes, this father's heart is broken as he hears his children cry.
There are moments when he thinks it would be better if they
died.
They cannot leave because they haven't any gasoline for the
car,
And yesterday he heard some news about a giant passing star.

Is that true, he wonders, because he's now afraid not to
believe.
How can he protect his family from a cosmic siege?

In fact his fears for his family are growing by the minute
And the ability to remain safe has far surpassed its limit.

The children can no longer go outside for the neighborhood is
not safe.
A father's heart is broken because his family is in this place.
A little food and a little water, a little light and a little soap;
These are precious commodities and the only thing more rare
is hope.

Then a soldier comes to his door and asks to speak with him.
He tells the father they are saved and a bus will come for them.
They family cries tears of joy for the children will get to eat,
And they won't die from the winter cold; they will have some
heat.

They all pack their bags waiting for the bus in anticipation.
When it arrives they quickly board without hesitation.
Their destination is unknown to them; but they don't really
care.
This appears to his broken heart as an answer to his prayers.

Of course he never was one much for praying, but he had been
as of late.

In fact, just like he did the watchmen, most preachers he would berate.

But now things will be ok; to the rescue has come the State.

As the bus arrives at the FEMA camp he soon will learn their fate.

This father was a good man; he just did not take heed.

This father was a good man and his family he longed to feed.

But this father did not provide his family's greatest need;

To have a father who believed God's Word and spent time on his knees.

The family has been separated, the children from the parents.

This facility is not what he imagined; it wasn't at all apparent

That the children would be sent away to undergo education,

And that even he and his wife would have to live in separation.

Every night his mind replays the words that he so long ignored;

The words of the prophets and the watchmen as they earnestly implored,

Warning good men and fathers to seek the God of all creation;

Preaching that we need repentance and the wise should make preparation.

None have left this camp; none have returned to their homes;
And in the Oval Office they have carried in a throne.
There is no one to represent those who have been interned,
And a father's heart is breaking as for his family he yearns.

This story continues to get darker and there is more that could
be told,
But you must seek the Truth for you today, for time will not
hold.
Time marches ever onward and every day the prophecies
unfold;
May the fathers heed the warnings and the children be
consoled.

To be prepared for tomorrow is not a difficult task.
To be forgiven of our sins, all we must do is ask.
Repentance is the preparation of the heart
And the heart is where the preparation for tomorrow starts.

A TOPSY-TURVY WORLD

Within this poem I touch on the fact that there are those who are attempting to open portals to other dimensions. According to Second Peter 2:4, fallen angels have been in chains below until the Day of Judgment. Could the opening of these portals unleash upon the earth what has been held in chains beneath the earth? I pondered that which is below coming above; hence a "Topsy-Turvy World."
These terms might need some explanation as well:
(1) Posse Comitatus–An act passed in 1878 which prevents the U.S. Military from being used by law enforcement against the citizens of the United States.
(2)Martial Law–The exercise of government control over the civilian population.
(3)Habeas Corpus–The protection we have against unlawful imprisonment.
Also, a phrase that appears often in my poetry is "the trading of truth for lies" found in Paul's letter to the Romans, and in that same letter Paul says there are those claiming to be wise who become fools.

A TOPSY-TURVY WORLD
by Randy Conway
Copyright © 2017

A Topsy-Turvy World seems a thing of fantasy,

But all too soon it will be our reality.

The laws of nature will become unhinged

And likewise will the minds of men.

Men groping about within a haze,

Ruled by leaders who are crazed.

———

Good will be called evil and evil will be called good
And absolutely nothing will remain as it should.

Unexplainable the things that will transpire,
Living in a world on fire.
Machines will seem to be alive
With unknown consequences of A.I.,
Becoming a world where lunacy will thrive.

The elitist proponents of Singularity
Continue fervently searching for immortality.
While at CERN it is the mad scientists' intention
To open gates to other worldly dimensions.

What will pass through these gates?
What will be our ultimate fate
When aberrations are given permission to enter in
And dwell within the realm of men?

Creatures once trapped in fairy tales
Will suddenly upon our world assail.
Even now in Ireland there is a search for gnomes and elves and
sprites,
And entertainment is obsessed with creatures of the night.

In days past there were giants in the land
And their return is nigh at hand.
The weather will be unpredictable
And we won't be able to define what's typical.

This unnatural world is given rise
Because we traded truth for lies.
For some, death will be their desire,
But they'll not be given a funeral pyre.

Others will long for life and fear their death,
But they will not be given breath.
There will be many unexplained mysteries
And a return of the barbarous acts of history.

Debt compounds and economies will not rebound
And money will be carried by the pound.
In a world that's Topsy-Turvy men will cry incessantly,
But in vain for mercy.

Things formerly given only an imaginary place
Will be thrust upon the human race.
And all the while Wormwood lies in wait…
But soon the unseen restraints that hold
Will allow the stars to fall upon the globe.

Destruction from the meteor swarms
And catastrophic solar storms;
Too many pulpits will remain hushed
As the world we know is being crushed.

The earth will shake and the lava flow
And incessant hot winds will begin to blow.
Even in the waters there will be fire
And in intemperate darkness this will transpire.
We must examine that to which we now aspire
Before our time has all expired.

Posse Comitatus will be revoked.
And Martial Law will be invoked.
Habeas Corpus will not last
And the Constitution–a thing of the past.

Feeding the frenzy of this frightening tilt
Is the now favored philosophy, "Do as thou wilt."

And the mantra of the illuminist, in case you didn't know,

Has always been and will always be, "As above so below."

To some this will seem just a silly rhyme,

But they don't know we're now on cosmic time.

A time where irreality is teeming

And the tangible is not discerned from dreaming.

How close is this Topsy-Turvy chaotic invasion?

It is now; we just don't see it because of our self-centered
hedonistic fixations.

It is the God of creation that gives to all things order

And our rejection of Him has allowed chaos to cross reality's
border.

Jesus has been and always will be the only shelter

In a Topsy-Turvy world of helter skelter.

ANCIENT GODS

This poem was written while listening to Steve Quayle interviewing Derek Gilbert on the Hagmann and Hagmann radio program. They were discussing Derek Gilbert's new book that I had been reading–"The Great Inception." I love the question Derek poses concerning his book: "Why weren't we taught this stuff in Sunday School?" Listening to these gentlemen speak on what I had been reading inspired me. The psyops of Satan is both ammunition and armor for today's believer. In today's world we need all the ammo and armor we can get! Understanding the Divine Council and small (g) gods as recorded in the Bible is monumental in understanding the Bible, understanding history and preparing for our future. "God stands among the Divine Council; He renders judgment among the gods."(Psalm 82:1)

ANCIENT GODS
by Randy Conway
Copyright © 2017

Ancient names from the past, names which have been ignored,

Are now revealed to be the names tied to our futures with a mysterious cord.

Ancient gods that we believed were just stories of myth and legend,

Now unveiled, the truth disclosed, the entities are real and not imagined.

Principalities and powers, rulers of darkness in heavenly places,

A strong delusion captures the masses and the lie that it embraces.

Those with eyes of the Spirit will see the ancient gods are still around

And the lies from Eden to Armageddon unfortunately still abound.

There are sacred places clothed in a mystical shroud,

Mountains where dimensions opened and beings dropped through the clouds.

The stories of old are come again and the future of man is threatened;

For the child of God there is victory, but we must utilize Spiritual weapons.

The Bible tells of the ben-Elohim and the princes of a Divine Council.

The days ahead will see the advancing darkness making groundswell,

But take heart for the transcendent God of all creation

Has prepared for those who trust Him, the parting seas of salvation.

You can think me foolish and a teller of fairy tales,

But as our history was, our future has been assailed.

Without the helmet of salvation you are exposed to a great inception;

Putting on the whole armor of God is a must, not just an ethereal conception.

ANCIENT VISITORS

Much of my poetry comes from listening to and reading the works of the great men of God that are appointed to this time in man's history. Deeper truths and better understanding are being revealed to us in greater or at least equal proportion to the continuing rise in depravity. God has not abandoned us to face the storms of this age alone; He promised not to forsake us. One of the great teachers that we are blessed with is Dr. Michael Heiser. His understanding of what took place on Mt. Hermon and the multifaceted purpose in Christ's ministry, sacrifice and resurrection is, to say at the least, eye opening. I am grateful for the scholars and researchers that God has blessed us with in order to teach us how to understand and live today and prepare us for tomorrow. Being neither a researcher nor a scholar I am humbled to take small portions of their great wealth of knowledge and write these small bite size pieces as I am inspired by their work and by the Holy Spirit. I have been amazed since beginning this new endeavor of writing poetry just how prolific both history and the Scriptures are with information, proofs and teaching concerning the fallen angels, their offspring, fallen angel technology and fallen angel religious practices. It is the history and the future of our world.

ANCIENT VISITORS
by Randy Conway
Copyright © 2017

Long ago on the top of Mt. Hermon a strange event took place;

Other worldly beings traveled through dimensions of time and space.

These visitors dwelt with men and sought the worship of the human race

Without regard for the consequences of leaving their first estate.

These visitors ravaged the earth, mankind and the beasts,
Siring unnatural offspring that eventually would on mankind feast.
The "gods," as they are known, bore giants history called men of renown;
Over the entire world their corrupted bloodlines could be found.

The life was always in the blood and the Watchers were not ignorant of this;
And their altering of DNA, by the Transcendent God was not missed.
There remained alive but one man whose blood had not been stained.
From His wrath and regret God's judgment would not be restrained.

Though the flood took the lives of those who were mortal,
There remained even after the rain those who had come through the portals.

There are those who prefer to think these are but grand stories or great mystery,
But many are the proofs, through the ages and through time, written into history.

The flood was not to be the end of this Great War for the worship of man.
On the plains of Shinar was unfolding yet another plan.
To reconstruct the events of Mt. Hermon, Nimrod with the Watchers was in collusion;
And even though Mystery Babylon has survived through time, Nimrod's efforts ended in confusion.

Then came another from a Heavenly dimension, but He came not through some celestial portal.
He came not as a Spirit, but born of a woman, to become an equal with mortals.
He came to redeem both the earth and the man;
Forgiveness of sin was only part of His plan.

He died between the heavens and the earth for our sin;
A free gift to all who into their hearts will invite Him in.
Now the reversing of Hermon has many perplexed,
But that is exactly what happened next.

You see, many of the lesser gods had been put into chains,

And Yahusha engaged them in order to explain

That they were defeated and there was yet for them further bane.

Then, rising to life, Yahusha proved He is the God who reigns.

While it is true that life is in the blood, it is only Yahusha's Blood that brings life.

Yet there still remains ahead more darkness, more battles and more strife.

There are still Watcher's and giants hidden in caves and darkness and under the ice.

First they appeared at Hermon, then Shinar and the next appearing will make thrice.

You may think this reads like some old fairy tale or some religious lore,

But the archeological remains in every corner of the world shout they were here before.

Neither alchemy, sorcery nor the mysteries of the ages will prevail in the final day;

And that day is not far, for the signs of the prophets are even now being displayed.

You can choose to believe or choose to reject; that privilege belongs to you.

Life and death are your choice so choose wisely, for the Word of Yahuah remains true.

Yahusha waits for the Father's command to ride and He will come with a flaming sword.

And all the preparations of the Watchers are for naught, for even Satan will recognize Yahusha as

The only King of Kings and Lord of Lords.

There will be a "new heaven and a new earth" and the Redemption Plan will be fulfilled.

The victory won at Calvary will be complete and the noise of the Watchers will be stilled.

The secrets of the Watchers are still kept within Luciferian Fraternities,

And those who follow their lies will find the reality of hell and eternity.

"Living He loved me, dying He saved me, buried He carried my sins far away.

Rising He justified freely forever and one day He's coming, Oh Glorious Day."

In the days ahead we will either Trust in "The Rock" or pray for the rocks to fall upon us.

It all depends on the choice you make today. So the question remains, "Who will you trust?"

CHOOSE YOU THIS DAY

Dr. Thomas Horn wrote an amazing treatise on the topic of Transhumanism and Conservative Eschatology for the American Academy of Religion, which was then included in his book, PANDEMONIUM'S ENGINE. He reveals that the amount of interest in transhumanism in the scientific community, the legal community, some religious communities and government agencies is shocking. The more you look into the transhumanist movement and pair it with the teachings of Scripture and many of the writers I have mentioned in these pages, the more you see this is nothing new. Solomon, the wisest man who ever lived, said there is nothing new under the sun. The altering of DNA, to change that which God created is a direct affront to God. It is contrary to His commands in Genesis when He said the earth was to bring forth living creatures, each according to its own kind. Transhumanism is a changing of the "kind." To understand the purity of bloodlines is to understand why the Scriptures take the time to list all those family lines. You know the ones — so and so begat so and so, who begat so and so — and on and on it goes. If Satan could have polluted the bloodline, Jesus would not have been the perfect sacrifice; the Lamb without spot or blemish. His plan did not work. God's did!

CHOOSE YOU THIS DAY
by Randy Conway
Copyright © 2017

Changing men into monsters is a dark and evil plan.

The Transhumanist agenda is to change what is a man.

It is not to improve our DNA but to alter the redemptive seed,

And those who cannot be redeemed are part of a hellish creed.

Can Artificial Intelligence be something beneficial,

Or is it to direct attention to things just superficial?

God's people perish for lack of knowledge of the things eternal.

The inspiration for these things was birthed in what Dante called The Inferno.

Fallen Angel Technology is being loosed upon this Age

And the one who sounds a warning is considered a fool rather than a sage.

There is a relentless lie that persists from Eden unto Armageddon;

This lie has proven to be one of Satan's most effective weapons.

Hitler, Hall and Pike, Bailey, Blavatsky and Kurzweil, all searching for immortality;

Transhumanist agendas thrive, looking for Atlantis, denying their mortality.

Through generations the lie has thrived and its adherents fought and clawed,

All believing the Nachash's lie that they could be as God.

From Eden to Armageddon nothing has or ever will really
change;
Men enticed by the serpent's lie that godhood they might
obtain.
The Blood of Jesus was shed to stop the destruction coming
from this lie;
It was for our forgiveness and our eternity the Son of God did
die.

Accept the Truth and live or reject the Truth and die.
Mock the Watchmen who point to Christ to your own demise.
Today is set before you an Eternal Choice of death and life;
The God of Truth, or the Father of lies that demands YOU are
sacrificed.

DO YOU SEE THE OCEAN IN THE SKY?

I have received emails asking what I meant by the title and first line of this poem, "Do You See the Ocean in the Sky?" The explanation is twofold. First, it is a reference to weather manipulation and the strange waves of clouds we see from chemtrails and HAARP activity. Secondly, the world is turned upside down; good is considered evil and evil good and is continually pushed by the progressives who seek a New World Order and Agenda 2030. As you read the poem below consider these statements and facts: From July 2016 until July 2017 the world experienced 38,992 earthquakes and the U.S. Geological Survey predicts that there will be 3.1 million deaths due to earthquakes in the 21st century. We now experience 35 volcanic eruptions per year. There have been 173 shooting incidents in the U.S. this year and this doesn't include civil unrest and riots. According to the U.S. Department of Veterans Affairs there have been 959,831 American deaths in the theatre of war since the Revolutionary War through the Gulf War. As sad as that is, it doesn't hold a candle to the losses incurred by abortion. When one looks at the deaths by abortion, it can only be described as genocide and holocaust. There have been 20,928,965 deaths by abortion worldwide from January 1, 2017 until July 1, 2017. There are an estimated 40-50 million abortions each year and I can't even fathom the number since Roe vs. Wade. If God heard the blood of innocent Abel crying from the ground, then the cry from the innocents murdered by abortion must be a deafening roar in His ears. This blood demands judgment and it will come. One can find endless articles on mind control, the revision of history, and the dumbing down rather than the educating of our youth. The Transhumanist agenda is really a continuation of Hitler's search for the Ubermensch and a longing for men to obtain immortality. Today 12% of the world's population suffers not just from hunger, but famine; that's 842 million people suffering. Of those, 9 million per year will die from hunger, starved to death. There are books written speaking of the signs of the blood moons and the alignment of the stars, and the Bible tells us in the book of Luke there will be signs in the sun, the moon and the stars. As you read below you will find all these things as described in this introduction. For Scripture references for this poem, see Revelation 6:12-17, Isaiah 24:20, Luke 21:25-26 and Matthew 24:3-44.

DO YOU SEE THE OCEAN IN THE SKY?
by Randy Conway
Copyright © 2017

Do you see the ocean in the sky,

The clouds in turmoil like a violent tide?

Can you feel the tension beneath your feet,

The faults of Earth waiting for release?

Do you see the evil men across the land?

Violence rules at every hand.

Can you see their disregard for Truth,

Regardless of all fact or proof?

Do you see the blood shed from endless war?

Of death by abortion; there is even more.

Can you feel the heat within earth's core,

Ready to release its molten store?

Do you see Transhuman monsters coming soon?

The powers of heaven shaken and men will swoon.

Can you see the perversions of every imaginable kind;

Perversions ruling hearts and obsessions ruling minds?

Do you see the arrival of the guillotines,

Brought to control those deemed "extreme?"

Can you feel the controlling of your thoughts;

What lies are now the children taught?

Do you see a day of hunger is at hand;

A want for food across the land?

Can you see from heaven the great signs

Proclaiming there is little time?

Do you hear the sound of the Watchman's cry

Warning all of what is nigh?

Can you hear the desperation in the Serpent's lies?

Do you see the ocean in the sky?

"He who has an ear, let him hear what the Spirit says to the churches. He who overcomes shall not be hurt by the second death." Revelation 2:11

ENSNARED BY TIME

Time. There are men who have devoted their entire lives to the study of time. There are sciences devoted to the research of time. There never seems to be enough time. We are intrigued by the thought of time travel and many block buster movies deal with the idea of time travel. The thought of aging has prompted an entire multi-billion dollar vanity industry to hold time back. There are workout programs, gyms to join, supplements to take, makeup artistry, cosmetic surgery and the search for the fountain of youth continues. We want faster travel in order to save time, and those things we would like to do, there never seems to be time for. The amount of time we each are given is not in our own control, but in the hands of God Himself. The Bible says we have an appointed time with death. For as much as we realize that time is limited, when it comes to eternity we always seem to think we have more time, or at least enough time to make eternal decisions. Despite our obsession with time, we still can't comprehend time because we cannot comprehend infinity. Time is eternal, and it will be time itself that will ensnare men when there is no more time for this age. (Matthew 24:44)

ENSNARED BY TIME
by Randy Conway
Copyright © 2017

Time–it is elusive, wasted, valuable, limited and limitless, but most of all time is persistent.

You cannot change time, you cannot speed it up or slow it down and you cannot alter an instant.

Men search for time, study time, long to understand time and they seek for time's beginning.
Men save time, waste time, wish to change time; some men warn our time for preparation is ending.

Time is a measurement and the measures of time range from nano seconds to millennium.
Each man is allotted his own measure of time; at its end his eulogy is a compendium.

Even the demons are aware of time and even the demons are constrained by time.
There were demons who spoke to Jesus saying, "Art Thou come to torment us before the time?"

Jesus spoke of a time that is coming, a time unlike any time ever seen before.
It will also be a time never to be seen again; some know this as truth, the foolish think it lore.

That hour is now upon us; this is more than speculation and this is more than mere cliché.
This is stark naked truth, with biblical proof, declared by the multitude of signs we see today.

Like a football game when there are but seconds left upon the clock;
The game is not over, but the quarterback takes a knee and the linemen cease to block.

Now this only happens when you are ahead in the game; it is limiting risk and being cautious.
If you're behind, caution is thrown to the wind and every effort made to minimize your losses.

There are now but seconds left on the clock that measures the Time of this Age.
It is time for the saints of God to fall on their knees; the call is now to pray.

Our Time is spent, we must repent and we must be prepared.
Time is persistent and unforgiving; those who ignore the call by Time will be ensnared.

"Therefore you also must be ready, for in an hour when you least expect, the Son of Man is coming."

FOLLOWING FOOTPRINTS

What can I say about FOLLOWING FOOTPRINTS except that footprints are left as evidence of someone who walked a particular route or path. This particular poem deals with the evidences left by the former races of giants. Stephen Quayle and Dr. Thomas Horn just released a new book that deals in depth with this topic entitled, UNEARTHING THE LOST WORLD OF THE CLOUDEATERS, Defender Publishing 2017. In fact, Steve Quayle has written extensively on this topic and he and Timothy Alberino have many documentary films on the subject. The entire GENSIX Company and True Legends Conferences are dedicated to the uncovering of the evidences of giants. I mention these gentlemen often as it is their research and published works that are the idea and inspiration behind many of the poems in this collection. As one grows in his or her faith and begins to discover that there are so many things that we weren't taught in traditional church or that have been westernized and lost in translation, it makes one hungry and eager to learn more. I am thankful for those whom God has placed it in their hearts to uncover for this generation those things that have been hidden or lost to us. I must also say that even though the ideas may come from these great men and others, the inspiration and the words come from the Holy Spirit and all honor and glory always belongs to God.

FOLLOWING FOOTPRINTS
by Randy Conway
Copyright © 2017

Footprints in the sand, footprints in the snow,

Footprints are left on all the paths wherever men go.

Footprints are found on the mountains men climb,

Our footprints are found in the records of time.

Footprints are found at the scene of a crime;

They mark out a path, a delineating sign.

Some footprints are quite short and others quite long,

Telling that men have come and where they have gone.

History records it and it seems rather odd

That there are footprints of giants who were mistaken for gods.

The foolish ignore them pretending they do not exist,

Yet the impressions are there, the evidence persists.

Footprints that tell of a race alien to us.

Footprints telling a story left in the dust;

A story that is scoffed, ridiculed and jeered.

What if the makers of those prints are still here?

Following footprints can be on occasion enlightening,

While following some can lead to the frightening.

There are footprints that lead to where blood was spilled;

Up a rough rocky mountain where redemption was sealed.

If I have left footprints the places I've been;

What do they reveal, my faith or my sin?

I will follow the footprints of the One I esteem;

They lead to a place where I am redeemed.

At the end of my life when my steps are retraced,

Only one path is preserved, because of grace the rest are

erased.

Footprints are left in the dust of earth's sod.

I choose to follow the footprints of God.

What footprints and path will you choose to follow?

If giants left footprints on the hills and in hollows;

If they are waiting in hiding and ready to strike;

What hope will you have against men of such might?

There is a path that is narrow and straight;

The footprints left there lead through a gate.

Only a few will ever find it, but inside it's safe.

Choose wisely your steps before it's too late.

HOW LATE IS THE HOUR?

Zephaniah 1:14 says, "The great day of the Lord is near, near and hastening quickly." In the book of Revelation the warning to us, "I come quickly," is repeated multiple times and the end of the age is likened to a woman giving birth. As the moment of birth nears, the labor pains come faster and faster with greater intensity. There are many writers and apologists who remind us of this fact, but I am inclined to join the warnings with the promise that He is able to deliver us. Without entering into an argument regarding when the Lord's return will be, or that we are not destined to wrath, or deep study in eschatology, I just want to point out the things in the Scriptures and the fact that we should be conscious of the warnings and the hour in which we live. Do we not live in a day when the profane is exalted? Psalm 12:8 tells us that, "The wicked walk on every side, when the worthless of mankind are exalted."

The reference in this poem to making the "bramble" a king is recorded in the book of Judges, chapter 9. After Gideon died, the Israelites made Baal-Berith their god; the ensuing bloody power struggle and the story of the trees looking for a king are described in Judges. It is the story of politics for every culture, every generation and every nation. It is our story. But regardless of how late the hour is, neither God's power nor His promises ever wane or diminish.

HOW LATE IS THE HOUR?
by Randy Conway
Copyright © 2017

How could I possibly describe the lateness of the hour?

What words would reveal God's deliverance or His power?

Is there a measurement small enough to measure the time till

God's judgment falls?

<hr>

120

Is there any language capable to articulate the might of Him
who created all?

Both are without measure–the minutia of time that now
remains,
And the immensity of power which the Living God contains.
Deliverance in the coming days is reserved for those who are
repentant;
Those who are clothed in righteousness, they will be the
Remnant.

The mockers and the scoffers and those who good despise
Will reap the whirlwind of God's wrath for clinging to their
lies.
The God haters and deniers that we have esteemed are in truth
but fools;
Good men by doing nothing allowed them position to impose a
godless rule.

Fools in their dedication to honoring depravity
Haven't considered that their choices bear tremendous gravity.
They have petitioned the bramble to be their king
And in the end the bramble will turn on them with a fiery
sting.

They will cry "peace and safety" but only find destruction
from which they will not escape.

The righteous man, by prayer and fasting, will live not by what
he sees;

He will live instead by Faith.

Signs have been displayed and warnings have been sounded,

And now we have choices we must make;

To perish with the fools or be delivered by God's power; your
future is at stake.

Alas the only sure future is in eternity and our time to prepare
for it is nearly past.

The past cannot be recovered and the choice you make today
could be your last.

Be not deceived for God will not be mocked and our sins will
come home to roost.

Seeds were sown to the wind…

And the hour is now upon us to reap the whirlwind that shall
be loosed.

Some in arrogance will stand their ground only to ultimately
fall.

Some will stand on powerful promises and answer to the call;

The call of One who stands knocking at the door, waiting to come in.

Peace and safety, deliverance and tomorrow are only found in Him.

HYBRIDIZED OR BASTARDIZED?

In an effort to not be redundant, since I have already made reference to the hybridization of mankind or transhumanism in prior poem introductions, I won't repeat it here. The only note I would add is that in the book of ENOCH, the Watchers who left their first estate and are responsible for the corruption of the DNA in the flora, the fauna and in mankind, were told by God through Enoch that they would receive no mercy and there would be no redemption for them. That is a harsh and frightening judgment; those who would seek to replicate the sin of the Watchers may find themselves also facing a harsh and frightening sentence. I'd think again before heading down this path.

HYBRIDIZED OR BASTARDIZED?
by Randy Conway
Copyright © 2017

Like putting together a puzzle and the pieces don't fit;

Just cut and paste and hammer and call it a double helix.

Is this not the science of fools and we call it genetic

engineering?

We will pay an awful price for the things that will be

appearing.

The puzzle pieces may stay in place, yet not depict the picture

intended by the designer,

But that matters little to those who seek their technology from

beings beyond Ursa Minor.

124

The race is on to be the first to successfully create a being fully hybridized;

As it was in the days of Noah, the seed line of God's creation will be bastardized.

And so it will be again that God will carry out the judgments that were prophesied;

A judgment so severe and grievous that were the days not shortened none could possibly survive.

Many will think this Hybrid Age is a wonderful advancement for man;

Only a few will know this is the repetition of an ancient evil plan.

When the Hybrid Age has become mature and dominates all life,

An ominous evil will be loosed and wickedness will be rife.

And rather than improving our world we will enter into a deadly strife;

Only the righteous will survive and only through the Blood of Jesus Christ.

IS LIFE SO CHEAP?

The following words of the prophet Ezra revealed the prayer he prayed for Israel, but I think it fits the world we live in right now. Before Ezra prayed he tore his clothes in an act of mourning as he considered the sins of Israel, especially its leaders and rulers. The Bible says that for a while Ezra just sat "astonished." Are we astonished any longer? Here is Ezra's prayer: "At the evening sacrifice I rose up from my heaviness and despite having my clothes and my robe torn, I knelt on my knees and stretched out my hands in prayer to the Lord my God and said: O my God, I am ashamed and embarrassed to lift up my face to You, my God, because our iniquities, have expanded over our heads and our wrongdoing has grown up to the heavens." (Ezra 9:5-6)

IS LIFE SO CHEAP?

How have we come to this, is life so cheap?

Are children garbage to be dumped in the street?

We murder babies in the womb;

Are mother's now prenatal tombs?

Infant sex and preteen whores,

Kiddy porn you can buy in stores.

Who will help to save the babies

From Molech and the arms of Hades?

America has now become
The full grown seed of Sodom.
Children sold and beaten, torn and bruised,
Forgotten, wasted, lost and used.

The Elite followers of Satan ignore the price
That God will demand for their child sacrifice.

Is there a champion among the sons of man
Who will stand in the gap against Satan's plans?
Will the abortionist continue to wield his knife;
Will the Luciferians continue offering sacrifice?
The people of God pray, "I lay me down to sleep,"
When we should be begging for mercy at Jesus' feet.

Never has the call for repentance been so great,
Never has the hour been so late.
Satan and his followers have now intensified their attack;
The innocent will pay if God's people continue shrinking back.

Selling the body parts of babies on the open market;
In all of modern history have the hearts of men ever been any
darker?
Their blood is on our money, their blood is on our hands,

Their blood cries from the grave and runs across our land.

"Please help the children" is what I pray:
"Keep them safe by night and day.
Take away the pain and dirt,
Kiss their sores and heal their hurt."

Father, forgive us for being a people who no longer blush and
are obsessed with sin.
We cry out in repentance, seeking for forgiveness before Your
patience has reached its end.

IT IS TIME

This poem is a pondering and list of my thoughts regarding the times in which we live. It is also about the events of our time and what our response as a Christian should be. 2 Timothy 2:11-13 says, "This is a faithful saying: If we die with Him, we shall also live with Him. If we endure, we shall also reign with Him. If we deny Him, He also will deny us. If we are faithless, He remains faithful; He cannot deny Himself." This verse says that there is a season, a time for every purpose under heaven ..." It is not enough to just ponder the times in which we live. We must realize that there is a divine plan in it all and that we are included in that plan. We must ask, "What is my calling for this time?" We are all called to be ready in every season to share the good news and we are all called to be watching in every season for we know not the day and the hour of our Lord's return. I must place one final caveat here: we are not all called to the same thing and we are only called to share what we have heard from the Lord or what He has given to us. (See 2 Timothy 2:2. Maybe you're called to pray. Find your closet and pray. Maybe you're called to preach. God will provide a platform for you. Maybe you're called to write or to be a good neighbor or called to support someone whom God has put on your heart. It doesn't matter what the calling. It matters that you answer the call, because now is the time!

IT IS TIME
by Randy Conway
Copyright © 2017

It is a time of uncertainty.

It is a time of disasters.

It is a time of weeping.

It is a time of calamity.

It is a time of hunger.

It is a time of war.

It is a time of mourning.

It is a time of want.

It is a time of depleting.

It is time for preparation.

It is time for gathering.

It is time for listening.

It is time for storing.

It is time for repentance.

It is time for revival.

It is time to be ready.

It is time to be restored.

It is time to be watching.

It is time to be armed

With the Armor of God,

With the Sword of the Spirit,

With expectation.

IT'S SOONER THAN WE THINK

I'm not pretending to be a prophet in this poem or to have some inside information that must be disclosed. I am only expressing the fact that there are biblical prophecies that declare there will be wars and rumors of wars and it is within our nature to often see things prophetic as far away rather than imminent. That can be a dangerous if not deadly mindset. As I have already written, we must be aware not only of the times we live in, but also the fact that time marches forward so steadily that we often don't see time encroaching or events approaching. Think about being on a great vacation with family and friends; time doesn't drag on endlessly, but rather seems to be over too quickly and it's time to return to work. The Bible says these events will sneak up on us like a thief in the night. Carol Burnett always closed her show with a little song that said, "Seems we just get started and before you know it comes the time we have to say so long." If you pay attention, even just a little bit, to the events taking place around the world and within the U.S., it is easy to see that war, even civil war in this country is a distinct possibility. This poem is a call to be aware and to be about our Father's business because the events of prophecy will come sooner than we think.

IT'S SOONER THAN WE THINK
by Randy Conway
Copyright © 2017

A war is coming and it's sooner than we think.

The signs abound, you can see we're on the brink.

But like so many before, I thought we still have time,

For on the brink could mean a thousand years, or so I was

inclined.

But God has given to me a word that came within my spirit.

The war is coming very soon; it was His voice and I could hear it.

I praise Him for His mercy and waiting for me to listen,

For what is now upon us is not a theory someone envisioned.

I asked, "What should I do, for I am not nearly ready?"

He told me just to stand with Him remaining true and steady.

So I will stand my ground with Jesus as my guide;

He is the only shelter when the nations all collide.

Now I'm expressing remorse for all the times I've strayed;

I'm praying every second for judgment to be stayed.

God promised to heal our land if we would humble ourselves and pray;

I am guilty of not doing my part, thinking it was not today.

I should have warned the people of God that gather in our churches.

But now it is much too late; even now the enemy searches

For his moment to strike, to bring us down, and I don't mean this nation.

He wants to bring under his authority–man– the prize of God's creation.

This war when waged will have a twofold battle line;
One line will be the physical war, the second a spiritual line.
The outcome of the physical battle will bring tragedy and strife;
The outcome of the spiritual one is the difference between death and life.

The outcome isn't only about the nations or which army is involved.
The outcome is about the bride of Christ and has the church evolved
Into the spotless bride arraigned in garments of pure white.
I don't know what God sees, but I have failed to shine the light.

I thank God now because He has shown mercy to me with grace
And I know it's not too late to earnestly seek His face.
So many Christians just like me love God and they believe,
But haven't spent the time to prepare by staying on their knees.

The church just loves to live by playing on the fringes of the world of sin.

Now is the time for Soldiers of the Cross to align themselves with Him.

Put on the whole armor of God and trust in Him to bring us through.

Repent of sin, trust in God and then stand firm is what we must do.

We cannot change the prophetic events that are yet to unfold.

We cannot change the hearts of men, not the young and not the old.

We can only check the heart that is our own to see that it aligns

With the Light that illuminates our way, the Light that from Jesus shines.

Let your fear be gone and loosen your bond with earthly things,

For His children will be safe when sheltered beneath His wings.

He is a rock, a mighty fortress, a strong tower to which we run.

I offer praise for His protecting love, to the Father, Spirit and the Son.

KEEP WATCH

This poem is an antiphony and carries a double message. The primary message is the message of Jesus to His disciples in Matthew 24:2-42, where He tells them to watch for signs of the end of the age. The second is a message of warning regarding the things, or in this case giants that are coming up on the earth and will cause men's hearts to fail for fear. I have said it often in regards to the "prepper" movement; the greatest preparation is the preparation of the heart. I have been teased by family members and friends over the years for always having the right tool or supply with me on a trip or even a simple picnic. I like being prepared. But if the soul is not prepared for eternity, all earthly and temporal preparation is really just a waste of time, money and effort, for "What does it profit a man if he gains the whole world but loses his own soul?" (Mark 8:36)

KEEP WATCH
by Randy Conway
Copyright © 2017

The disciples called out to Jesus saying, "Look, look," as they

gazed at the magnificence of the Temple.

But Jesus replied in a surprising way saying not to "look," but

to **"watch;"** it is that simple.

Inescapable evidence saying the world is rampant with giants.

Continuing in His instruction there comes a warning we have

heard, but ignored the words,

"When you see…"

This instruction is not limited to the men of old, it comes
through time to us; we must **watch** in
order to see.

From the darkest and deepest places they appear.

Continuing in desperation the world cries out in its delusion,
"Look, look here."
And the day will take them unaware and men's hearts will fail
for fear.

*What does your heart say; what is that feeling in the bowels of
your soul?*

The day is not known. The time is not told. The particulars
remain … a mystery.
What can we do? How can we prepare? The instruction is
simple. **"Keep watching."**
Therein is our victory.

Will you be ready? They are ready!

We must **watch**, but what are you watching? Where are you
looking? A ghibli encroaches.

Who are you watching? The question is raised, are you
        watching? For the Day of the Lord
approaches.

Hungry. Lunging from the darkness. Assaulting.

KEEP WATCH!

ONE MORE PERSON

Normalcy bias has crippled large numbers of the population,
so that even when they hear the truth they are inclined to reject
it. With so many infected with this mindset you might wonder
why the preacher keeps preaching and the Watchmen continue
crying out when it seems no one is listening. There are a few
reasons: First is because they are called and the Scripture lays
out the responsibility of the Watchmen. If the Watchman warns
and his warning is ignored the Watchman is free of guilt, but if
he refuses to warn there is blood guilt upon him. Secondly, the
apostle Paul teaches in 2 Corinthians 3:6-7, "I have planted,
Apollos watered, but God gave the increase. So then neither is
he who plants nor he who waters anything, but God who gives
the increase." To not continue speaking the truth would be to
assume the place of God, or to know the mind of God as to
who will respond to the call. Finally, they understand that it is
God's will that none should perish and you could be the one
that responds to the Truth. "So it is not the will of your Father
who is in heaven that one of these little ones should perish."
(Matthew 18:14) They are crying out for just one more person.

ONE MORE PERSON
by Randy Conway
Copyright © 2017

The Bible tells of 4 riders of the apocalypse, yet there are those

who these accounts wish to disprove.

The Heavens and Earth may pass away but the Word of God

will always remain true;

And the unbelievers will run in vain from the riders as they are

trampled by their hooves.

The Gates of Hell have been opened and chaos has come through the Gate.

There will be no order out of this chaos; only more chaos, murder and hate;

And the New World Order Pundits are looking now to take their places as magistrates.

Because it's never happened before the world believes it won't happen now.

The words and warnings are ignored and soon the unbelievers all will bow

Before a ruler they never chose and the sheeple will question, "How...

How did this happen? We did not know that things would be this way."

The watchmen grow weary yet they continue to speak and they continue to pray

That one more person will hear their words and one more person will be saved.

PREPARED?

Ordo Ab Chao or Order Out of Chaos. According to the website, Zero Hedge (www.zerohedge.com), this is the doctrine that runs the world. Order Out of Chaos provides a scapegoat for the masses and they don't consider where the chaos originates; the masses only look to the one offering solutions to the chaos. Even for those of a non-spiritual persuasion, the agnostic or hard core atheist, if you're aware or as some put it "awake," then you realize the continual presence of the Hegelian dialectic being practiced within the realm of the ruling elite. In short, this is a social issue as well as a spiritual issue. Saul Alinsky's book, RULES FOR RADICALS, has become the holy scripture for those who desire not to be public servants but to own power and influence for themselves or their favored agenda. How often have you heard Rahm Emanuel quoted over the past few years as saying, "You never want a serious crisis to go to waste." The conspiracy theorists and government trolls jump on every event that hits the news and call them "false flags" to the point that it is becoming harder to determine what a false flag is and what is an actual event. The false flags exist, but the hearts of men have become so black that they are not only capable of, but actually do commit atrocious acts of violence on a daily basis. Then there are fear mongers who profit from instilling fear, while those who earnestly try to warn are quickly grouped with the profiteers and the warnings then become lost in the chaos of blogging and chatter. Occam's Razor states that the simplest explanation according to the evidence at hand is usually the correct answer for any given problem. Therefore, given the fact that the Bible says we are to always be watching for we know not the day or the hour of our Lord's return, and considering the amount of Scripture dedicated to describing the "Day of the Lord" and the end of the age, I say being prepared is the correct action and answer to the question of the hour in which we now live.

PREPARED?
by Randy Conway
Copyright © 2017

There are those who don't believe that the future offers any
threat;
They ignore the words of warning to their own suffering or
maybe even death.
But what of those who do believe that tomorrow holds the
possibility for peril?
Are they prepared to survive the chaos when societies become
feral?

I have heard of men who have food stored in massive
quantities,
And if famine is in the future they could possibly survive that
calamity.
But I must profess that even though they have food to spare
These men are not actually prepared.

There are those with guns and bullets, knives and swords;
If roving gangs attack, they might hold off a hungry horde.
But even though their guns are loaded and their aim is steady,
Like those with food these men are not really ready.

A practiced few could cook a meal and heat their home with a
flint stone and some sticks;
Some have water and stored up medicines to survive a drought
and treat the sick.
A very few have bunkers and a nuclear event they are prepared
to face,
But for the reality of what is ahead they are not adequately
braced.

There are those who can name all the nations in the BRICS
Alliance;
They're watching the Middle East and globally any nation
governed by a tyrant.
They stay abreast of all the news so they cannot be taken
unaware,
But information alone isn't enough to consider yourself
prepared.

Bug out locations and hordes of cash, gold and silver too,
In an economic catastrophe might get you through.
But through to what is the question that must be asked.
How long could a family last?

Now, having a supply of food is indeed a wise and prudent
thing to own,
And a man with mettle is becoming rare — one who protects
his family and home.
Having all these things might show wisdom, prudence or for
some a little fear,
And the Watchmen continue warning that something big is
near.

All of these solutions are limited to only disasters natural in
origin.
What about the spiritual events just beyond the sight of normal
men?
How will you prepare for a world of converging dimensions?
What in your storehouse will make you ready for evil's grand
ascension?

Too many ignore the warnings given by the prophets and
through the Word;
Others prepare, but in ignorance, for their spirits have not been
stirred.
For both the coming Day of the Lord will take them as a thief
in the night,
And what of the man thinking he will escape because the
rapture is in sight?

Those who claim to be the Christian of Psalm 91 are plenty,
But what if they are called to be the ones from Revelation 12
or Revelation 20?
Also in the pews are fools who won't prepare, misquoting
verses from the 13th Chapter of Romans,
And to their folly they are unprepared, ignoring the truth of
Biblical omens.

Why is repentance the preparation that stands far and above all
the rest?
Because we will all stand before God Almighty, not just
endure the coming tests.
Are you covered by the Blood of the Lamb? What is the word
of your testimony?
Did you ignore the Watchmen God has sent or horde your
provision for you only?

Preparing for the natural is needed and the wise hear a warning
and take action.
Beyond the natural the preparation cannot be an all too late
reaction.
For men will say, "But in Your Name we did great and mighty
things for You."
Sadly the unprepared will hear the reply, "You I never knew."

Too many are preparing only for calamity or disaster.

Preparation is imperative for time is moving faster.

But if you're not on your knees in confession and repentance,

Then you are not prepared, for we will not face just disaster; we are going to face our sentence.

Words cannot tell of all the things that in our immediate future lay.

We cannot know who will live or die or which men might be saved.

But this I know if you desire to be prepared for the coming brutality,

You must be prepared to face God's judgement…not just a calamity.

REDEMPTION DRAWETH NIGH

Everything in the following verse is taken from real (not fake) news. You can find articles on every topic covered in this poem, with the exception of a flood that covers Iowa. It's hard to find a rhyme for Samoa. For example, in 2009 an earthquake caused a tsunami in Samoa leaving 189 people dead. The 2011 earthquake in Japan is still in the news, being one of the worst quakes in history with 16,000 casualties and 100,000 people displaced from their homes. The Fukushima Daiichi nuclear power plant is still dumping toxic radioactive water into the ocean and we may see the impact of this disaster for many years. This poem reflects on how difficult it is to know the truth concerning the earth's climate. Climatologist, Michael Mann, who is best known for his "hockey stick" climate models, is in contempt of court in Canada for refusing to provide court ordered data. It is expected that a ruling will come soon stating that Mann acted with criminal intent to commit climate fraud. How few are the real climatologists and how many are the climafrauds and climagendists? As for the rest of the points pondered in this poem, they are common knowledge to anyone with a radio, television, smart phone or internet access. In Luke 21:25 Jesus tells us what the world will look like just before the coming of the Son of Man. "There will be signs in the sun and the moon and the stars and on the earth distress of nations, with perplexity, the seas and the waves roaring..."

REDEMPTION DRAWETH NIGH
by Randy Conway
Copyright © 2017

A tsunami in Samoa,

An earthquake in Japan,

A flood that covers Iowa;

Elsewhere lava runs across the land.

Muslims telling lies preaching love is Allah's will;
All the while they teach their children how to maim and kill.
There is a nuclear threat that is coming from Iran,
While terrorists are still finding shelter in Afghanistan.

So many lies, how can we know?
We're told the earth is warming
While others say it's getting cold;
Both sides sounding out their warnings.

Rockets and bombs so frequently land on the Israeli state;
They're launched on a daily basis by those who harbor hate.
Around the world power hungry politicians try to divide God's
land,
Playing into the Luciferian, Illuminati New World plan.

The dollar is now in a perpetual state of deflation,
While the price of oil persistently stays in fluctuation.
Stock markets perpetually spinning completely out of control,
While businesses and banks are continuing to fold.

We want government support of gender confusion,
But we mustn't allow any religious intrusion.

———

That would infringe upon the hallowed separation;
Another of the enemy's favorite creations.

With false prophets saying I'll plant you a seed,
They are only pandering to our own growing greed.
We have politicians claiming to be our savior.
In all of history has our condition ever been any graver?

The media spouts its biased spin.
The world ignores the trouble it's in.
Each new day brings new disaster.
The ignorant hoping someone has the answer.

Those telling the truth are limited in their speech,
While evil abounds and continues to increase.
Do not be discouraged but look up to the sky;
For the believers, redemption is now drawing nigh.

War and famine, flood and fire;
Sexual perversion growing dire.
Attacks in and on the church without hesitation;
Schools are flooded now with Satan's infiltration.

Incessantly dead babies are crying from the ground;

Sadly it seems that everyone ignores the sound.

Righteousness and truth rarely can be found,

And we deny that judgment is quickly coming down.

How long will this depravity last?

Will any for atonement ask?

One day soon we'll hear a trumpet blast;

Our redemption now is coming fast!

The clouds will be rolled back like a scroll;

A rider descends through a gaping hole.

The world will analyze this situation

As prophecy unfolds its revelations.

Society and nature are now in turmoil;

Religions and nations are in war embroiled.

I am looking to the Eastern sky

Because my redemption is drawing nigh.

The birth pains have moved into full blown labor.

We need to daily proclaim our Savior.

Banish any thoughts of fear

Because our redemption is almost here.

Like a thief in the night to the unaware;
Now is the time for the bride to be prepared.
The One whose name is Faithful and True
Says, "Behold for I am coming soon!"

REST ESCAPES ME

*On her website, www.whygodreallyexists.com, Meranda
Devan has categorized and listed many dreams and visions
from believers around the world, sharing with the public what
God has revealed to them through dreams. The book of Joel
which details the "Day of the Lord" tells us that in the last
days "...your sons and daughters will prophesy, and your old
men will dream dreams, and your young men will see visions."
It seems to me this is happening with greater frequency and
because of the connectivity of the internet we are able to share
more information, including dreams and visions, than ever
before. In his book, DEVIL TAKE THE YOUNGEST, author
Winkie Pratney describes the war on childhood and reveals
the occult roots of that war. The roots go back to the evil spirit
of Molech and run through history with the mystery religion of
Babylon and Babylon's ruler, Nimrod, of whom the Scripture
tells us began to become a gibborim, altering his DNA. The
fallen angel religion can be followed through the Middle East,
Europe, Asia and the Americas, and will take you from Aztec
Ziggurats to UFO's. One of the ancient places of worship to
Baal was in Palmyra, Syria. An arch stood there built by the
Romans so that worshipers would pass through the arch on
their way to the temple dedicated to Baal. A replica of that
arch has made its way around the world during what was
called, "World Heritage Week," being placed in Dubai,
London and on September 19, 2016, New York City. It is
considered "heritage" to honor Baal, but if New York were to
erect anything to honor or commemorate the Living God of the
Bible, we would surely hear the cries of separation! The
commandments would be, and have been vandalized and
destroyed, and the courts be filled with law suits over honoring
God!*

REST ESCAPES ME
by Randy Conway
Copyright © 2017

It seems as of late rest escapes me; I sleep, but rest has become elusive,

For in my sleep the terror of my dreams is relentlessly intrusive.

Is it fear in these visions of the night or just an increasing anticipation;

Like warnings that require my attention of an approaching abomination?

This loss of rest continually attempts to undermine the surety of my peace.

I stand firm in faith, for the loss of peace will give to chaos a burgeoning increase.

I wake and look about my room to find assurance that I am still there,

And call upon the Name of Jesus to break the increasing tension in the air.

Pondering then what I have seen within my dreams, making careful assessment

Of the condition of my heart, and in repentance I make a total investment.
If the dreams of the night are a window allowing me to peer into tomorrow,
Those things I've seen are scenes of trouble, war, hunger, debasement and sorrow.

Then I looked at the evening news and realized these things no longer reside only in dreams;
Lewdness and perversion is commonplace and the filth of hell is sent live stream.
Morality is totally abandoned and we teach kindergarten children about same gender sex;
And with sorcery, vampires and zombies the whole world seems to be obsessed.

I pinch myself to see if I am asleep while the threat of war comes closer with each passing breath.
The entire world is now at war and I wonder when the streets will be filled with death.
No longer is it nightmares but "awakemares," for we are now in a world that gives honor to the profane.
The politicians that we trusted and elected are hiding their hands so we don't see their bloodstains.

Demon possession and demonic influence is on the rise.

There is unexplained phenomenon in our skies,

And every day 115,000 innocent unborn babies die.

It is no wonder that rest escapes me when I close my eyes.

The fires of Molech have been ignited and are burning bright.

There is an obsession with Hitler and the spirit of the Reich.

The spirit of Antichrist is alive and the Dragon is swishing his tail;

In major cities around the world evil is erecting its temples to Baal.

What will follow the building of a temple to a pagan god?

Will the people gather at the burning alters with shouts of praise and loud applause?

Whether awake or in dreams the heaviness of the hour cannot be evaded;

Still many will not prepare and many will not repent, because truth for lie has been traded.

The Elite are stocking the pantries of their underground hideaways.

The economy is failing fast; in fact it is in a state of total decay.

Jesus warned us in the Bible not to be deceived or caught unaware.
Some feel the tensions of the night and are awakening to prepare.

But if you try to share the message that we should make preparation,
You will become discouraged and met with violent accusation
That you are a fear monger or a Bible thumper, and the masses want no part
Of your "conspiracy theory." They only want to know when the next party is going to start.

The party has been started and the temples will be built to the breaking of God's heart.
The message of repentance is ignored and the church offers its parishioners a menu A La Carte.
When I ponder these things from a physical perspective it seems to me it's time to be prepared.
When I question the state of society from a spiritual perspective, I know it's time to be in prayer.

Destruction waits in Babylon at the Temple of Baal and Judgment day is here.

We must "keep watch," not close our eyes and hope that evil disappears.

Preparation is a work that we must do because the time of battles has now come.

Those who fail to repent and prepare will by the powers of this world be overcome.

SOWN IN WEAKNESS, RAISED IN POWER

The entire 15th chapter of 1 Corinthians deals with the resurrection of Christ, the resurrection of the dead and the resurrection body. Paul teaches that it is the promise of eternal life and the promise of resurrection that removes the fear of death. This poem is a call to not become discouraged but to hang on to the promises of God. We are called to fight the good fight, to endure until the end and to work until Jesus comes. Sometimes that is hard and we just need a little encouragement along the way. For those who are not familiar with the silence in heaven and the trumpet blast, see Revelation chapter 8 for the source of those lines. Be of good cheer and let the weak say I am strong.

SOWN IN WEAKNESS, RAISED IN POWER
by Randy Conway
Copyright © 2017

Sown in weakness, raised in power,

Bearing the likeness of earth;

Soon to bear the likeness of heaven,

Many will sleep but all will be changed.

Men are continually sowing to the wind

And even now are reaping the whirlwind of their sowing.

The humble, the faithful, those sowing to the Spirit,

Their promised harvest is eternal.

Oh, but weariness is attempting to overtake the faithful;

This is a warning to remain vigilant, brush off the weariness.

Due time must pass but the harvest will come;

It is only in the proper time that the harvest is seen.

They are considered blessed who persevere.

Even as the farmer waits for the land to yield its crop,

So the only Righteous Judge is standing at the door, waiting.

Standing firm is imperative because the Lord's coming is near.

Many others will come; they are clouds without rain,

They are shepherds feeding on the sheep.

They are trees without fruit, foam on the waves of the ocean.

Soon Heaven will be silent, silent for half an hour.

Then you will smell the aroma of incense.

Fire comes from heaven, rumblings, lightning and earthquakes.

What is the sound I hear? Is it a cry? Is it a shout; a moan?

No, It is a distant trumpet!

Again and again the blow of the trumpet is carried on the winds.

Seven times the sound pierces space and resounds with haunting echo.

Hail and fire, the sea turns to blood; be steadfast.

Celestial bodies fall from afar striking the earth. The faithful are holding on to promises now.

More than I can tell and yet, even more horrors await. It is the reaping of the whirlwind!

How long now must we persevere until the seeds of the righteous are ready for harvest?

We must brush off weariness again.

We will remain faithful, preparing to bear the likeness of heaven, to be the bride of Christ.

In the proper time redemption will be seen. Seeds now sown in weakness will be raised in power!

STARGATES

For those who are aware of what took place atop Mount Hermon and understand what is being attempted with the LHC at the CERN laboratories in Switzerland, you will understand the following poem. Many great researchers and scholars have covered the topic of Stargates. I have already made reference to Steve Quayle, Dr. Michael Heiser, Derek and Sharon Gilbert, and Tom Horn. Let me add to this list L.A. Marzulli, Anthony Patch, Josh and Christina Peck, Dr. Michael Lake and John Baptist. A simple internet search of the works of any of these individuals will quickly reveal to you the information that would not be silenced in me and that inspired the following poem. There are many other great writers and "Youtubers" that I haven't the room to mention here or this book would end up being just a lengthy list of recommended reading. I pray that I don't offend any by the absence or the inclusion of their name. I only mention them to say the poems included here are not from spicy pizza before bed, but the result of reading and listening to real research and real biblical exegeses by many godly people.

STARGATES
by Randy Conway
Copyright © 2017

As gravity increases and time folds, a passage is opened to an unknown dimension.

To those who know, it is a gateway, though some deny they're real and consider it science fiction.

But fiction has no empirical proofs or eyewitness testimony.

The writings of antiquity testify the truth, not hypothesis.

———

161

Beware! The opening of these gates will bring a global apostasy.

Educated fools play with these passageways thinking they are in control,
But they see not the portentous threats that lie behind the blackness of these holes.
Many have come and many have gone, but still we search for the keys
That will allow us to open the gates that lead to mystery.

Now there has been much talk and speculation that governments have found such gates,
And they are willing to shed much blood or even go to war to keep their secrets safe.
Authorities around the world guard the ancient sites,
Hiding or denying the existence of what was moved in the dark of night.

Stories, myths and legends are told, passed down from ancient tribes;
Tribes from every tongue and nation whose stories all describe
An ancient race of giants and the pathways through which they fly;

An ancient race of hybrids that desire to see all flesh die.

The believers intently watch the signs to be prepared for their return.
The scoffers remain ignorant and choose not to listen or discern
The words of the prophets giving warning or the evidence that abounds,
While the elite are guarding secrets hoping the truth is never found.

For you see, the truth cannot be found out by the masses or the general population;
That might set the masses free and we must be kept in mass sedation!
If the truth were preached and the people reached there could be mass salvation,
And that would hamper Satan's plan for the New World Order aberration.

There are beasts that come with the opening of dimensions, creatures we cannot see,
And Satan's minions are seeking personal greatness through evil loyalties.

But their greatness will not be long lived for the beast is but an incarnation
Of a defeated fallen angel that will one day be forced to make proclamation

That Jesus Christ is the only one True King of Kings and Lord of Lords.
If the gateways are opened, will we then see the foretold Day of the Lord?
Men remain in denial of the judgment of the Lord, and they reject His Word;
They are too afraid to see the truth and so they call the truth absurd.

Now those things which God buried in the deep waters of the flood,
Were buried to cleanse the earth and to protect the seed within the blood.
The seed remained protected and Jesus came to redeem the man.
He offers to all eternal life and those who accept Him are covered by His Hand.

If you are not covered by the Blood of Jesus Christ,

When the gates are opened you are at risk of life.

Men must seek the Truth while it may be found;

The cost will be too great when the evil has been unbound.

The stories, myths and legends have an ancient foundation and are not just passed down orations.

The true watchmen are not barkers spouting lies to dramatize and create a great sensation.

Those who hide the truth are not our great protectors; they hide behind lies for personal elevation.

The clues of time and the clues left on the earth reveal the truth of the former altered mutations.

Now I am prepared to make a multi-dimensional journey through a gate that is straight.

There are thieves and robbers who will attempt to do the same through their hidden Stargates.

Unfortunate for them they will not travel through, but that is not to say the gates will not be used.

Many will come through to rule all men, and tribulation will then be loosed.

THE LIE FROM EDEN TO ARMAGEDDON

The twisting of Scripture is a favorite ploy of Satan and our lack of knowledge of the Scripture always works to his advantage. Lies are best implemented when mixed with a little truth and Satan is both the master and father of lies. So, when we get half-truths from those who are in positions of reporting the news, preaching the gospel, teaching the Bible or elected to represent us, and it is with intent, then the person telling the half-truth is serving the master of lies. It has been said that a half-truth is a whole lie. The wisest man that ever lived said that there is nothing new under the sun, and so it is with the lie that we can be as God. It was told in Eden and will persist to Armageddon.

THE LIE FROM EDEN TO ARMAGEDDON
by Randy Conway
Copyright © 2017

In the beginning, in the garden where the man and woman dwelt,

There was a Nachash–quite beguiling–and the Nachash felt

That he should be as God and be worshiped as the same;

And so he approached the woman in order to play his little game.

Now it was to the woman a little lie was introduced

And by this lie the man and woman were both seduced.

From the serpent's heart came the lie and the woman was then awed

To think that by disobedience she too could be as God.

———

166

From this early beginning the lie began to spread

And generations throughout centuries on this lie have fed;

From pharaohs to Caesars, from Kings and Queens and even pawns,

All have harbored in their hearts the desire to be as God.

Hitler, Hall and Pike, Bailey, Blavatsky and Kurzweil all searching for immortality,

Trans-humanist agendas thrive looking for Atlantis, denying all mortality.

Through generations the lie has thrived and its adherents fought and clawed,

All believing the Nachash's lie that they could be as God.

From Eden to Armageddon nothing has or will ever really change;

Men enticed by the Nachash's lie that godhood they might obtain.

The Blood of Jesus was shed to stop the destruction coming from this lie;

For our forgiveness and our eternity the Son of God did die.

There is no truth in Satan's words from the garden to today;

It is his goal to be as God and those opposing him he will slay.

The fear of death is relieved only through the cross,

And those who continue to believe the lie remain eternally lost.

THE OPENING OF DEADLY DOORS

Around the world there exists thousands of ziggurats, pyramids and sacred mounds all with specific astrological significance and precise alignment. The ancient cyclopean building and architecture is not limited to a single geographic region. There are sacred places, tunnels, caverns and relics that all insist that this world was once inhabited by a race of giants with technology far beyond our own. While we may all agree that pyramids and ziggurats are unique and hold special significance, likewise so do mountains. Michael Heiser in his book, THE UNSEEN REALM, refers to mountains and gardens as the dwelling places of gods and provides both historical and biblical proof of this fact. In the Hayu Marca Mountain region of southern Peru, an area referred to by the locals as the "City of the gods," is the "Puerta de Hayu Marca;" the gate of the gods/spirits. Some say it is a dimensional portal that many have attempted to open. On the border between Israel and Syria stands Mount Hermon, which has been considered a holy mountain for eons. It is called the secret dwelling of the Anunnaki. The Apocryphal book of Enoch tells of 200 Watchers that descended on Mount Hermon in the days of Jared. Men realized the significance of this mountain and have attempted throughout history to recreate it with pyramids and ziggurats and mounds. In the land of Shinar, the most famous of all ziggurats was built by Nimrod. The tower of Babel was the place where Nimrod sought to re-create the activity of Mount Hermon. There are ziggurats and pyramids in Egypt, Mesopotamia, Meso America, Mexico and Central America, China, Europe and North America. Cultures such as the Aztecs, Mayans, Toltecs, Mongolians and Native American have them too. But, this is not a book for that purpose. I just want to emphasize the fact that these places do exist, they have monumental significance, and the history of these places is our future. Today, there is a place where men

---

and women are still trying to replicate the events of Mount Hermon; that place is called the "Large Hadron Collider."

THE OPENING OF DEADLY DOORS
by Randy Conway
Copyright © 2017

Mountain top to mountain top,

Ziggurat to ziggurat,

Dimension to dimension;

Who traversed them and with what intention?

From the heavens to the earth

What atrocities were given birth

When the ben-Elohim saw the daughters of men,

And in that moment an evil enterprise did begin?

From battle to battle into the flood

The seed had been stained, a corruption of blood.

Therein lies the intention;

It was an evil contravention.

From the Adamite world until our own

The god-men and their offspring have been known.

Most thought them but fable and myth or story;

A few might have given them the place of allegory.

Ancient peoples in the Americas and around the globe

Knew of the Watchers and the giants that roamed.

They knew of the portals that bend time and space,

Allowing dimensional beings to mingle with the human race.

But did they know how ancient was this plan,

Always attempting to corrupt the seed of man?

To stop the Savior from ever being born

Is why the ben-Elohim crossed the heavenly bourne.

From the Vatican to Washington

Is but Abaddon to Apollyon.

From Cydonia to Sardinia, into the Smithsonian,

Once again something wicked this way comes.

Are the OOParts remnants left by ancient giants, the Rephaim?

The question must be asked, "Are the giants coming back again?"

The evidence is mounting proving their return is imminent;

Untold peril will await all those who are ambivalent.

There are legends, lore and stories told

In books and parchments and ancient scrolls.

Clues are left behind in rocks and caverns and under the ice;

Many are the seekers of power the evidences have enticed.

Cover-ups and lies attempting to guard the truth from our sight;
Are the things of darkness now being brought into the light?
Is there power or fallen angel technology to be obtained?
Can man survive that which under the earth is chained?

The ancient portal doors long closed, men now long to open,
Using technology mixed with spiritism as druidic chants are spoken.
Watchmen warn this could bring an unimaginable giant holocaust,
As hungry cannibal cyclopeans are released when this line is crossed.

From ancient Mayan to the Hopi the stories differ little;
In Europe and China ancient people received the same transmittal.
And so it is as the accounts of giants span the globe,
In every age, in every land the giants found abode.

From Giza to the Valley of Elah, Goliath was not alone.
Can man survive the days ahead if giants are released to roam?

The connecting thread through the stories told is of giants eating flesh.

It was not the flesh of animals that satisfied the hungry Gilgamesh.

From Switzerland to Washington men are searching for the key,

From Babylon to the Smithsonian to unlock the Stargate that sets them free.

Is the fifth world now upon us, has timed now turned another page?

Will this be the generation to witness the "Cloudeaters Golden Age"?

"Be strong and courageous," is the command to the believer.

"Move along. Nothing to see here," is the lie given by the deceiver.

He who knows the beginning from the end is able to keep the repentant,

But for those who scoff the Living Word, the unimaginable is for them impendent.

THE WORLD IS FULL OF GIANTS

Having amply introduced the idea of giants in previous introductions, this poem needs no preface except Genesis 6:4, "The Nephilim were on the earth in those days and also after that, when the sons of God came in to the daughters of men, and they bore children to them. These were the mighty men of old, men of renown."

THE WORLD IS FULL OF GIANTS
by Randy Conway
Copyright © 2017

"And there were giants in the earth in those days."

This is not myth or fiction; this is what the Scriptures say.

The men of old who became the men of renown;

The evidence of their exploits can still be found.

"As it was in the days of Noah so shall it be."

What could these words mean to you and me?

Did not the giants of Noah's day feed upon men's flesh?

How will we survive a world of ubiquitous Gilgamesh?

Denial makes us comfortable and we believe if we ignore

The words of the Scripture and the prophets repeated o'er and o'er,

That the events to come can be called just another theory

And things can be laughed away by calling them conspiracy.

Giants, we believe belong in myths or legend or lore.

They're acceptable if kept in story books and movies but nothing more.

We are too consumed with admiring the work of our own hands

To see the things of mystery and prophecy moving across the land.

The disciples of Jesus were enamored with the Temple and its construction;

But while they we're saying "Look," Jesus said to "Watch," there is coming destruction.

That destruction is upon us; we did not see it coming and the seed is now corrupt.

What miscegenation has changed our seed; what gateways have been opened and what will next erupt?

What did Enoch know and what ancient words have been ignored?

What runs the mountains of Mexico that has never been seen before?

What is seen along the highways, the backwoods and forests of the world?

What shall be our fate when the Zam-zum-mims are exposed and the truth has been unfurled?

We MUST watch. But what are you watching? Where are you looking? The Emim approaches.

Who are you watching? The question is raised for the Day of the Lord encroaches.

Transhuman or nonhuman, birthed or made, matters little if Rephaims can walk free.

Repentance is the only preparation, for truly "As it was in the days of Noah so shall it be."

THE RIDER ON A WHITE HORSE

*"I saw heaven opened. And there was a white horse. He who
sat on it is called Faithful and True, and in righteousness he
judges and wages war. His eyes are like a flame of fire, and on
his head are many crowns. He has a name written, that no one
knows but He himself. He is clothed with a robe dipped in
blood. His name is called The Word of God. The armies in
heaven, clothed in fine linen, white and clean, followed Him on
white horses. Out of His mouth proceeds a sharp sword, with
which He may strike the nations. 'He shall rule them with an
iron scepter.' He treads the winepress of the fury and wrath of
God the Almighty. On His robe and on His thigh He has a
name written: KING OF KINGS AND LORD OF LORDS."*
John the Revelator (Revelation 19:11-16)

THE RIDER ON A WHITE HORSE
by Randy Conway
Copyright © 2017

John saw the heavens open, he was allowed to peer inside.

The sky rolled back like a scroll opened and gaping wide.

He saw a rider mounted on a horse with reins held tightly in

His hand.

John the revelator said, "He was the Son of Man."

His hair was white as snow and His eyes a blazing fire.

He is the one who's coming to bind and chain the liar.

His feet were bright as bronze and His voice like mighty ocean

waves;

From His mouth there comes a Sword and in His hand 7 stars that stay.

His face John could not see because it's brighter than the sun.
He is the first and last, the one who died and is now the Living One.
He holds the keys to death and to the grave.
When John saw the rider he fell down, shaken and afraid.

The rider of this horse is named Faithful and True.
On His head will be crowns; many not a few.
A name was written on Him and only He knew what it meant.
The Mighty One of God and from the Father sent.

His robe was dipped in blood and His title the Word of God;
He comes to tread the winepress of the wrath of Almighty God.
On His robe and on His thigh written words which strike an eternal chord;
There for all to see is written "King of Kings" and "Lord of Lords!"

THE FINAL WATCHMAN

*"For thus the Lord has said to me: Go, station a watchman;
let him declare what he sees." (Isaiah 21:6) "...Watchman,
how far gone is the night? Watchman, how far gone is the
night? The watchman says, 'The morning comes and also the
night...'" (Isaiah 21:11)*

THE FINAL WATCHMAN
by Randy Conway
Copyright © 2017

One by one the Watchmen

Are leaving their places upon the wall.

One by one the Watchmen

No longer voice their call.

One by one the Watchmen

Are leaving to find a sheltered place.

One by one the Watchmen warn,

Those choosing to ignore now have sealed their fate

When the final Watchman

Leaves his place upon the wall,

When the final Watchman

No longer sounds the warning call,

When the final Watchman

Is released by God to flee the Watchman's station,

When the final Watchman

Is silent, then time is gone for preparation!

RANDY CONWAY

American poet, Randy Conway, has written hundreds of poems and his verses have been read on national and international radio talk shows. Conway is best known for his series of poems that cover powerful observations on subjects such as End Time prophecies, religion, government corruption, patriotism, life's struggles, worship and life and death. His long-awaited collection of End Time poems has been shared on Steve Quayle's website and also on many other websites such as Millennium Ark Preparedness, Conservative Read as well as read on the Hagmann and Hagmann Report radio show.

Randy Conway became a poet after a successful career in business, but as his poems continue to gain world-wide exposure he has entered a new phase of his artistry. This is his first book of a multi-volume book collection, and there are many more poems, videos and books in the works.

Conway is a voice to the voiceless millions who are seeking hope, strength and encouragement in life. The simple power of his verse is relatable to the masses who respect The Creator and who seek a way of expressing their feelings about the world in which we live.

Find more of Randy Conway's works online at:
randyconwaypoems.com
Randy Conway Poems on youtube.com
Randy Conway Poems on facebook.com

To Contact Randy Conway:
Write to:
P.O. Box 157
Halltown, MO 65664
Or email at:
randyconwaypoems@gmail.com

61615369R00117

Made in the USA
Columbia, SC
25 June 2019